M000084662

GET
EPIC
SHIT
DONE

GET EPIC SHIT DONE

ANKUR WARIKOO

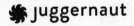

juggernaut

JUGGERNAUT BOOKS
C-I-128, First Floor, Sangam Vihar,
Near Holi Chowk, New Delhi 110080, India

First published by Juggernaut Books 2022

Copyright © Ankur Warikoo 2022

10 9 8 7 6 5 4 3 2 1

P-ISBN: 9789393986078
E-ISBN: 9789393986085

All rights reserved. No part of this publication may
be reproduced, transmitted, or stored in a retrieval
system in any form or by any means without the
written permission of the publisher.

Typeset in League Spartan by
R. Ajith Kumar, Noida

Printed at Replika Press Pvt. Ltd

Dedicated to all my teachers,
most of whom do not even know me.

When the student is ready, the teacher appears.

– Lao Tzu

CONTENTS

INTRODUCTION

I started my first book, *Do Epic Shit*, confessing that it may very well be the most useless book you will ever buy. My second book could give it competition. Because it is full of the one thing I hate in life – prescriptions!

Remember those exciting headlines that never fail to seduce us?
'3 Things All Billionaires Do First Thing in the Morning'
'5 Ways to Find the Love of Your Life'
'7 Ways to Crack Your Dream Job'
'9 Ways to Find Out If You Are Smart. You Won't Believe No. 3!'
All of them have a common theme.
They make us believe that there is a path to life.

That there is something, a method, a process we are unaware of.

And once we are made aware of it, we will accomplish everything we have wanted to.

You know what?

It isn't true.

There are no prescriptions in life.

There is no one way to live it.

Each one of us builds our own path, our own way, our own journey.

Then why am I writing this book?

This past year you have asked me many questions. Questions which I have tried to answer using my experiences.

How do I manage my time?

How do I deal with failure?

How do I make friends?

How do I decide on my career?

How do I love myself?

This book comes out of our conversations.
I have written it in a question-and-answer
format. Questions asked by a student.
And answers given by a teacher.

36 life questions.
36 answers to those life questions.
And 36 possible times you assume that only
these answers are the right ones.
They are not.
They are my answers.
And they worked for me.
They might not work for you.
However, I do hope my answers drive you to
yours.

I have had many teachers in my life.
Most of them do not know me, though.
Their answers led me to my answers.

That is the joy of learning.
It can happen at any time, at any place and
for anyone.
Should you be willing.

DO EPIC SHIT was all about provoking you. Getting you to think. Getting you to reflect. Getting you to question.
GET EPIC SHIT DONE is an attempt to get you to act.

So whenever in doubt, open the book to the question you have and go through the answer. If it helps you come up with your answer, the teacher will have appeared!

PART 1

MANAGING YOUR LIFE

How Can I Stop Comparing Myself to Others?

Student: Why is the world around us designed in a manner that we are good only when we are 'better' than others?

Teacher: We fall prey to such comparisons because we have built our worldview on two false assumptions instead of understanding the basic facts of life.

Student: Which are?

Teacher: The first incorrect assumption is that the world is a zero-sum game.

Student: What does a zero-sum game mean?

Teacher: It means that for one to win, another has to lose.
If my score is +1, your score has to be -1, so that the sum is zero.

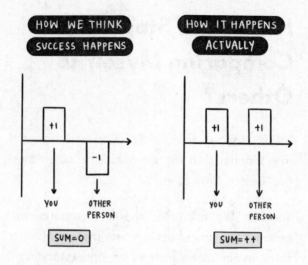

Student: Isn't that true?

Teacher: Far from the truth.
As a matter of fact, all of us can create as many wins for ourselves instead of waiting for someone else to lose.
The world has abundant opportunities.
Look at it historically and you will realize this.
Look at India itself. Our parents' generation had it really hard. Their parents had it harder.
In contrast, we sit on so many opportunities that they never experienced.

Student: That is such a beautiful way of putting it. Does it mean that instead of fighting for a bigger slice of pizza, I can have as many pizza slices as I want?

Teacher: Only metaphorically, yes :)

Student: Sounds interesting! What was the second incorrect assumption you were alluding to?

Teacher: It is a fact that all of us come across very different opportunities.
Which means, by default, we will all end up at different places because we started off differently.

Think of it this way: there is no one, absolutely no one on planet Earth who has the same characteristics as you do.
Your temperament, your capability, your choices, where you were born, your family, your upbringing, your luck – all are so unique to you that by design no one can be like you.

Since everyone started off differently, everyone by default will end up differently.

Student: Reminds me of the Taylor Swift song lyrics: You're the only one of you, baby that's the fun of you!!

Teacher (smiling): Yes!

Student: But I must confess this is hard to put into practice. When I see someone doing well, all I see is that someone else is winning and not me.

Teacher: This is what I ask myself when I see someone else winning:

If they earn more than me, will that be true forever?
If they have a job and I do not, does that mean I will never have a job?
If they happen to be in a lovely relationship, does that mean I will be lonely forever?
The answer to all of these questions is no.

Student: That's helpful. But really not. I still feel I am not winning.

Where do I find that peace at that moment?

Teacher: The emotions that we humans go through are not permanent. What we feel today, we will not feel tomorrow.

However, what we feel today can either make us depressed or induce us to take action.

You see a friend with a good job and you don't have a job?

Use that emotion to work harder to get a job.

Student: This sounds so easy to do! Yet why don't we end up doing it?

Teacher: Because there is a deeper layer we have not yet uncovered. Ask yourself the following questions:

'Why am I feeling bad?
Because they are doing well and I am not.'

'Why do I feel that?
Because they have a job and I don't have a job.'

'How is that a bad thing?
If I do not have a job, it means I am not making money to fulfil my needs and wants.'

'If I do not have a job now, does this mean I will not have a job ever?
Of course not, I am capable. I can get multiple jobs; it is just a matter of time and patience.'

'Then why does someone else's job make me feel so bad about myself?
Perhaps to me, they are successful and I am not.'

'Is that the only definition of success?
Maybe. I do not know.'

'Once I have my own definition of success, do I think I have done everything I needed to do to get there?

No, not at all.
'I could still work harder. And better.'

'What's stopping me?
Me!'

When you have this dialogue with yourself, you will be surprised to know that your definition of success is not clear to yourself.
These emotions will lead you to introspection, help you create a definition of success.
Does this mean you will stop comparing yourself to others? No.
It simply means that when you do, you will know what to do next.
Dig within.

The worst use of your time is comparing yourself to others.

Student: Instead of having imaginary conversations with others, the way is to have real conversations with yourself?

Teacher (smiling): The teacher has appeared!

How Do I Build My Communication Skills?

Student: I struggle to communicate my ideas, my thoughts. I get nervous. I feel anxious. What can I do to improve my verbal communication?

Teacher: First, understand that our ability to communicate verbally is a direct reflection of our ability to structure our thoughts clearly. And that begins by writing!

Student: Writing? Oh please!
I am not a writer. Nor am I interested in becoming one.
It is the last thing I would do.

Teacher: Hear me out.
Writing is the slowest form of expression that we have as humans.
We think fast.
A lot of us tend to speak fast as well.

Writing can never match that speed.
Which is actually the reason why writing is so effective.

When we write, we are training our brain to select the most important thought out of all that is inside it.
That process trains us to control the pace of our thoughts, structure those thoughts and refine them.
So when we write, we essentially tell our brain – this thought is the most important. Let me write it down.

Student: Oh, I see. That makes sense. Is there a minimum amount I need to write? When should I write? What should I write about?

Teacher: Write every day.
Start with a page. You don't have to go beyond that in the beginning.
Write about anything at all.
The only thing is to draw a conclusion.

Every time you have written something, end with the sentence: 'This tells me that . . .'

The conclusion brings it all together.

Writing daily is not just for writers.
It is for communicators who wish to express themselves better.

Student: How so?

Teacher: It ties your thoughts together.
To begin with, when you start writing, your thoughts will be all over the place.
And if you end with just that, it will not help you infer a point.
This ending sentence trains you to move towards a conclusion.

Imagine the same process translating into your verbal communication – you speak towards a conclusion.

That is what you want, eventually, isn't it?

Student: Precisely.
But it cannot be just that. Writing alone can't make me a good communicator.

Teacher: It is a necessary step but not the only step.

The next step after writing will be to practise speaking.

With writing, your thoughts get structured. But they still lack the emotions that your voice can generate.

So I advise my students to record a video of them speaking for a minute, for 90 days straight.

Play back the video.
Make a list of all the moments where you erred. Think of how you can do better.

And then come back the next day to work on the errors.

Student: Awesome.
That sounds like a task, but I like that it is just a minute a day.
Does this really help?

Teacher: Anything you do consistently will help.
I had a student who took this advice to heart and recorded 365 videos every day for a year.
You would not recognize the person in the 365th video from the first one.
Just one year.
In a life of several decades, just one year can change your life.
That is the beauty of this practice.

Student: I would love to be her in a day's time.

Teacher: You would but cannot do so, not in a day.

As you practise, I also want you to observe the speakers you like the most.

Watch their videos.

Pick up their style.

Make a note of all the things that you find appealing about them.

Imbibe them.

As you do so, ask yourself: How can I bring their emotions into what I say?

Student: No shame in copying, huh? I like that.

I also see a lot of effective communicators projecting a sense of confidence that is not verbal.

They do not sit with closed arms.

They rarely play with their hair or hands.

They do not shake their legs.

Do these things matter?

Teacher: Of course.

When people close their arms, it tells us they do not want to listen and are married only to their own opinions.

Shaking your legs is an expression of nervous energy.

What we don't speak speaks louder than what we do.

Did you know that body language consists of 55% non-verbal communication, tonality consists of 38% and words only 7%?

Student: Wow!

That is why the same thing said by different people has a different impact on us.

Teacher: True. And it's even more important in today's world.

Because a lot of our communication happens over electronic media, we cannot always see each other's body language.

Thus, the choice of our words and how we weave them together becomes so much more important.

The only way to get better at it is to read.

The more you read, the more you help your mind form the right structures, use the correct sentences and articulate better.

Student: So writing and reading, both are important for effective verbal communication. That already sounds like a lot of work.

Teacher: Oh, you haven't even reached the hardest part . . .

Student: Wait, sorry to cut you, I wasn't listening. Where do I learn the skills of body language from?

Teacher: The hardest part of communication is listening.

Student: Sorry, what?

Teacher: The hardest part of communication is listening.
Something that you aren't doing right now.
Understandably so.
Because it is hard.

We often listen with the intent to reply. Not to understand.
And that makes us impatient communicators.
Have you ever been in a conversation where

you said something important only to hear a completely unrelated answer that set you wondering if they were listening?

Student: So many times!

Teacher: You now know why.

Student: I realize being an effective communicator is not so much about speaking English fluently or acting confident. It is simply about understanding the emotions of the person you are communicating with.

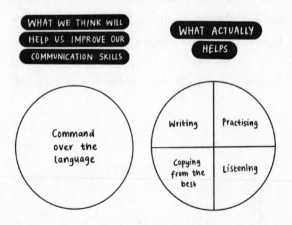

WHAT WE THINK WILL HELP US IMPROVE OUR COMMUNICATION SKILLS

Command over the language

WHAT ACTUALLY HELPS

Writing | Practising

Copying from the best | Listening

Teacher: You are so right.

Of course, please do not dismiss the power of knowledge, the power of preparation, the power of practice.

All these are critical to any delivery – verbal or written.

But despite all that, many falter.

Because they never care to understand the person they are communicating with.

Student: Thank you. This gives me a lot of direction.

And I wanted to apologize for cutting you in between your sentences, because I wasn't listening. I will be mindful of this from now on.

Teacher (smiling): The teacher has appeared!

How Do I Build a Growth Mindset?

Student: I hear a lot about growth mindset versus fixed mindset these days. Aren't we all born with a fixed mindset about who we are and our capabilities? Is it even humanly possible to grow beyond the mindset we are born with?

Teacher: I believed that for the longest time. Growing up, I was convinced that people are born with a fixed capability.
I stand a changed person today.
Our capability isn't fixed.
Believing this truth is part of the growth mindset.

Student: Is it because of the fixed mindset that most people do not achieve beyond what they think they are capable of?

Teacher: Yes, absolutely.

Which is why we must understand the growth mindset and how to build it.
To build the belief that your capability is not bound by anything.

Student: Is that really possible? Isn't it difficult?

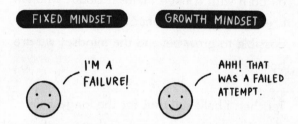

FIXED MINDSET   GROWTH MINDSET

I'M A FAILURE!   AHH! THAT WAS A FAILED ATTEMPT.

Teacher: There are three ways in which a growth mindset is established.
The first one is to spend time with people who are nothing like you, in a disciplined manner.

When you spend time with people who are nothing like you, you stretch your fixed mindset to have a wider perspective.

Student: But why should I spend time with people who I do not agree with?

Teacher: Just because you think you are right does not mean someone else isn't.

Spending time with different people does not mean leaving aside who you are. It simply means seeing the world differently from the way you do.

For example, if you are an engineer, a whole lot of your thought process is shaped by your qualification and training – about zero and one, black and white, bits and bytes, what works and what doesn't.

But when you spend time with someone pursuing art or social sciences, someone who is taught that life is not zero or one, and is instead a continuum, someone who sees the world as a spectrum of grey, instead of categorizing it as black and white, what do you think would happen?

Student: The way they see the world is drastically different.
And I will get to see that?

Teacher: Correct!

Because there are multiple avatars of the same thing we call truth.

Once you ask yourself 'what do they know that I do not', you open your world to more possibilities than before.

Student: This was very useful. What is the second way of establishing a growth mindset?

Teacher: It is about understanding how risk plays a part in shaping your life.

Student: But isn't risk equivalent to losing, and thus something to avoid?

Teacher: That is a trait of a fixed mindset because it assures stability of the status quo. Whereas, those with a growth mindset understand risk instead of running away from it.

For them, risk is not a limiting factor but, rather, an opportunity.

Student: Whenever I think of risk, I think of stock market investors losing money.

Teacher: I understand.
Here is what might help.
Stock market investors understand the market and how it functions.
They know that in the short run of 6 to 12 months or even 1 to 2 years, the market will go up or down, and may even give negative returns as against fixed returns of fixed deposits. However, they also know that over 5 to 10 years, the market will beat almost every fixed-income instrument.

It applies to most things in life.
For example, changing your career, forming a new relationship or investing your money.
You need to understand that you cannot eliminate the risk.
You can only understand it.

Student: So people with a growth mindset kick their comfort zone and understand the risk?

Teacher: And in understanding the risk, they become who they are – growing human beings in action!

This brings me to the third and final point of cultivating a growth mindset – living without a sense of entitlement.

Student: But I have worked hard to get where I am!
Do I not deserve to be entitled?

Teacher: The mistake most of us make, that keeps us fixed in our mindset, is to believe that we deserve to be where we are in life.
That we have worked hard to achieve this.
The truth is we are just plain lucky.
Plain lucky!

We were lucky to be born into a family that gave us food, shelter, an upbringing, education and values because of which we sit on privileges that most people won't even get to experience for a second of their lives.

Most of them work far harder than we ever will.

Most of them are smarter than we will ever be.

Yet we trick ourselves into believing that we deserve to be where we are.

And that makes us entitled.

Entitled people don't grow.
They wait to be grown!
Because they believe the world owes them everything they desire.

Student: Should I neglect my hard work altogether?

Teacher: Realize that where you are in life is as much by luck as it is by hard work.
The ones with a growth mindset think of growth and gratitude as their lifestyles.

Thus, when they achieve something, rather than feeling entitled, they feel grateful.
That gratitude serves as a fuel to achieve more, replacing that fixed mindset feeling of standing in front of the mirror and saying, 'I deserve this!'

Student: So, if I spend time with people who are nothing like me, it will broaden my horizon. If I think of risk as something to be understood and not eliminated, I draw the courage to act beyond fear. And if I do so in a manner that I am never entitled, I ensure that I grow in the process.

This guarantees I am never limited by my self-imposed idea of what I am capable of doing.

Teacher (smiling): The teacher has appeared!

How Do I Make Tough Decisions in Life?

Student: I often wonder how some people make big decisions with ease. I get confused while making not just big decisions, but also small ones like which T-shirt to order online.

Teacher: What's the worst thing that would happen if you ordered the incorrect T-shirt?

Student: I'll return it and order another one?

Teacher: Can we do that with big decisions in life as well?

Student: Won't that be risky?

Teacher: Tell me something, have you ever ordered a wonderful T-shirt that looked perfect online, something that would be your go-to T-shirt for the rest of your life, and when it arrived, it simply didn't look good? Have you ever been through that?

Student: Several times.

Teacher: What did you do then?

Student: I returned it.

Teacher: What does that tell you about decision-making?

Student: Maybe, the fact that we can get back to square one if the decision does not work out.

Teacher: That is the beautiful thing about most decisions.
Most of them are reversible.
Which means that if the decision we take doesn't work out, we can always go back to where we started.
The sad part is that most people think that their decisions are irreversible.
So they spend an inordinate amount of time figuring out the 'perfect' decision!

Student: Shouldn't that be what we do? Reach that perfect decision?

Teacher: Which brings me to the second part of making decisions: You will never know whether the decision is right or wrong unless you've made it in the first place!

Student: But if I make the wrong decision, will that not waste my time?

Teacher: But the act of not making a decision is in any case wasting your time. You are so hooked on finding the right decision that you are actually not taking any decision.

Student: Then how do I navigate this?

Teacher: When you want to make a tough decision, you evaluate all the parameters that are important to you between all the available options. Say you want to decide between College A and College B. We will make a list of things that are important to you and assign them the weightage in order of their importance.

Item	Weightage
College reputation	40%
Course I study	20%
Placement opportunities	10%
Peer group	15%
Methodology of learning	15%
	100%

The reason we have assigned weightage to each one is that you may not have equal importance for every parameter.

Once you have done this, you will then rank both colleges with 1, 2 or 3 points – 3 being the best, and 1 the worst.

Item	Weightage	College A	College B
College reputation	40%	2	3
Course I study	20%	3	1
Placement opportunities	10%	1	2
Peer group	15%	2	2
Methodology of learning	15%	2	3
	100%	2.1	2.35

Based on all these parameters, we conclude that it would be wise to get into College B. So, we will make that decision.

Student: But can't I simply go with what someone else in my family has already decided?

Teacher: That would be an unwise thing to do. They are different people with different mindsets, different contexts, who want different things from life.

Everyone differs on how important are the individual parts. Which is why the choices we make are all so unique.

Student: But then what if my decision doesn't work out?

As you said, what if I realize that only after I have made the decision, i.e., after I have picked my college and started studying there? Picking a college is not a reversible decision!

Teacher: Which brings me to the Stoic principle of decision-making. Once you have figured out which decision to take (without knowing whether it's the right one or not), imagine the worst-case scenario when you take the decision.

What could be the worst thing to happen? Imagine it vividly as if it was happening right now, in every bone of your body, and ask yourself: 'Will I be okay despite that worst-case scenario?'

Before you decide on the answer, ask yourself if you have asked all the difficult questions.

Will I be okay financially? Mentally? Emotionally? Spiritually? Physically? Socially? If the answer is yes, then take the decision.

Remember, there is no way of knowing whether it is the right decision or not.

What you have done through this exercise has prepared your mind for the worst-case scenario.

The fear around the decision is what you are focused on.

Not the decision itself.

Student: What if the worst-case scenario is something I won't be comfortable with?

Teacher: In that case, you may not be ready for the decision.

You have two choices then.

Either wait to take that decision, which may not always be possible.

Or

Make a plan to face the worst-case scenario.

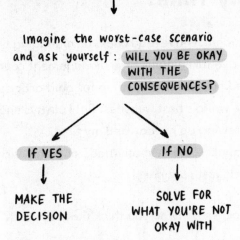

WHEN YOU'RE UNSURE OF A DECISION

↓

Imagine the worst-case scenario and ask yourself: WILL YOU BE OKAY WITH THE CONSEQUENCES?

If YES → MAKE THE DECISION

If NO → SOLVE FOR WHAT YOU'RE NOT OKAY WITH

Student: So, instead of losing sleep over the right decision, I should take the decision I want to take and figure out what to do if the decision does not work out for me.

Teacher (smiling): The teacher has appeared!

How Do I Manage My Time?

Student: I have read books on managing time; I have taken many time management courses and have even signed up for paid articles on the world's best websites. But I always end up screwing up my day and my time.

It makes me demotivated, and the vicious cycle just continues!

Teacher: Why do you think that happens?

Student: It happens because I do not know how to manage my time well! I know what to do but I still don't do it.

Teacher: If you feel the books, courses, videos do not help, why do you still engage with them? Do you think the courses or motivational videos or books teach you something that you don't know?

Student: My hope is they will teach me something new.

Teacher: There isn't anything new to be taught in time management. Every book, course, video will end up saying the same thing. Managing time, my friend, is a very personal endeavour. We all have buckets of time when we are the most energetic, when we are the most productive and when we need to slow down.
Our first step in managing time is to understand our relationship with time.

Student: Relationship with time?
What does that even mean?

Teacher: If you do not understand how time works for you and your relationship with time, you will always struggle to manage it.

You will be able to manage your time only when you understand your relationship with it.

Tell me, do you know what you did last week? How did you spend your time?

Student: Mostly, I prepared my to-do lists, but they hardly got accomplished.
Even if I want to keep track of time, it just slips away. So, the answer is no, I do not have a track of how I spent my time last week.

Teacher: When you reply to that question, you are focusing on the time you spent working towards something that you were meant to work on. That would be not more than 30–50% of your entire day.

Student: I know, but to me, it looks like the entire day!

Teacher: You would have also spent your day sleeping, eating, doing things outside your work or even wasting time. However, very often, when we think about time, we only think about what we're supposed to 'do', instead of our entire life.

Student: But isn't our entire life centred around doing things?

Teacher: It is, which is why you have to start measuring your time to understand your relationship with it. As hard as it may sound, it will mean measuring every single thing that you do in your day (for at least 10 days, ideally 30 days), right from the time you wake up to when you go to sleep, and account for two questions:
a. Why did you do what you did?
b. How did it make you feel at the end of it?

These two places of awareness will then tell you what changes need to be made. Answer these two questions, and you will begin to understand your relationship with time.

Student: This sounds like hard work. Is this what all good time managers do?

Teacher: Nope.
But that is how everybody starts.

Think of the first day you rode a bike or drove a car. You were conscious of everything that was happening to you, very aware of the shifting gears, the cows in front of you, the cars and people coming in your way – you were totally present and observant.

Today you're a pro, riding, driving – without a thought to what's happening around you – listening to music, biting into your sandwich, talking to your friend, even daydreaming :)
That is the power of habit.

I remember recording every hour of my waking day from age 13 to 26. For 13 full years!
So today, I don't have to. I know exactly how I spend my day. It is a subconscious habit now.

Student: So if recording every hour sounds overwhelming, that is just the initial hiccup? Over time, will it become a subconscious habit such as driving?

Teacher: Absolutely.
This is the early effort that you will have to put in so that you don't have to do it for the rest of your life.

Student: I still have a reservation.
Does it mean that I must have zero hours of wasting time? I work for a certain number of hours a day and I take small breaks. But I would also want to waste time watching Netflix and chilling with friends. I love doing that. To make up for the lost time, should I optimize my workflow?

Teacher: That's a very practical question.
Literature on the principles of time management wants you to be 100% productive. But that is rarely the case. We should also not strive for that.

Think of time as an allocation.

Allocation between 4 types of tasks that are:
- Not urgent and not important
- Important but not urgent
- Urgent but not important
- Urgent and important

Then ask yourself: What combination of these tasks makes me the most productive during my day?

For example, you may feel extremely productive by taking five-minute breaks every 30 minutes. During those breaks, do whatever you want. Read a book. Take a short walk. Chat with your friends. Anything *you* want.
That gives you the energy to return to work and do a good job.

However, if the five-minute break every half an hour becomes two hours, you feel shitty at the end of the day for wasting time, even though in the moment you felt good. That allocation then doesn't work.

Only when we know where our time is spent in this matrix can we finally start making the shift towards a quadrant of our choice.

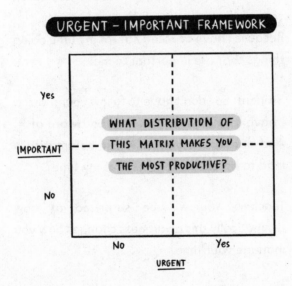

URGENT – IMPORTANT FRAMEWORK

Yes

IMPORTANT

WHAT DISTRIBUTION OF THIS MATRIX MAKES YOU THE MOST PRODUCTIVE?

No

No   Yes

URGENT

This idea is not mine, nor is it new. It is called the Eisenhower Matrix. The difference, however, is that the matrix tells you to eliminate ALL the things that are neither urgent nor important. I am suggesting that you should live with them and find a balance that works. For example, 13% of my weekly time lies in this quadrant. And I like it that way. During this 13% I waste my time. But it works for me. Why? Because I have taken care of the remaining 87%.

Because I have devoted 75% of my time doing things that are important to me.

Student: So I don't have to follow your matrix. I have to build my own. And be aware of it. And once I am aware, will it automatically lead to better management of my time?

Teacher: You will be surprised at how dramatically this awareness changes how you manage your time.

Student: And once I have understood that, I will know what to do next, right?

Teacher (smiling): The teacher has appeared!

How Do I Focus?

Student: I lose focus easily.
I may be working on something that will pay my bills, but something else on another tab will catch my attention, be it a text from a friend or pictures of someone's vacation on Instagram or even an email to attend to! It is so easy to lose focus!

Teacher: When you say lose focus, is it because what you're doing is not interesting, or is something else more interesting?

Student: To be honest, of course, something else is more interesting, even though what I'm working on is important.

Teacher: This is very normal human behaviour – where we are working on something that we have to do, but there is something else that is exciting, seducing and perhaps even more interesting!

My question to you is: Why do you want to fight it?

Student: Why shouldn't I? That seems like a weird question.

Teacher: What if I tell you that wasting your time and letting your mind wander should be a part of your schedule?

Student: Are you being serious?

Teacher: Yes, I am! The minute you designate a time as wasting time, your brain is no longer interested in chasing it. It already anticipates it!

The brain now knows that at, say, 12.30 p.m. you have 'wasting time' scheduled for 30 minutes. Which means, it is no longer a forbidden fruit that you have to resist. But rather something you give yourself as a reward for your focus thus far.

Student: That seems cool. Very, very cool. However, I'm unsure if doing that would actually help me focus more!

Teacher: Let me explain to you with an example. Did you know that having cheat days in a diet schedule helps the body get closer to fitness?

When someone is very disciplined on a weight-loss journey, their body also looks forward to the reward foods. And when they know that they can get it on some specific days by eating whatever they want (not going overboard, of course), the body adapts to the weight-loss journey faster. With more effective results!

Student: Oh, so scheduling a reward instead of running away from it makes the pursuit of discipline less mundane?

Teacher: And more fun :)

Student: Does that mean I am allowed to watch dancing cat videos as soon as I wake up?

Teacher: You have to earn that wasting time, my friend.
Putting in the disciplined hours is the currency to earn that wasting time guilt-free! Otherwise, you are training your mind and body in the incorrect direction.

Student: Oh. At what point of time can I actually jump into wasting time, knowing that I have earned it?

Teacher: A wonderful way of doing it is the Pomodoro Technique. It's a scientifically proven technique, which suggests you divide every interval of 30 minutes into 25 minutes of work and 5 minutes of break.

During that break, do whatever you want. Check your phone.

Talk to your friend.

Take a walk.

But after those 5 minutes, you are back to work for the next 25, and so on.

After four or five such cycles, you take a longer break of 30 minutes.

Rinse and repeat.

The 30-minute cycles ensure that they give the mind the 5-minute break it's craving for.

The break, in turn, is a recharge to return to work for another 25 minutes.

It is crazy how effective this technique is once you start practising it.

Student: Can I also use the Pomodoro Technique of focusing and time-wasting when I am working on something extremely hard? Will my mind not want to pick up that task in the first place?

Teacher: When the temptation to waste time is maximum because you are going to work on a difficult task, is when this technique works its biggest wonders!

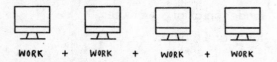

WHAT WE THINK BRINGS FOCUS

WORK + WORK + WORK + WORK

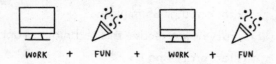

WHAT ACTUALLY BRINGS FOCUS

WORK + FUN + WORK + FUN

Student: Won't it mean I'll put less effort into the task??

Teacher: Think of having two tasks in your kitty. One is something you do not want to pick up because it's difficult, and the other one is something that doesn't require a lot of effort.

If you pick Task 1, your mind will actually look forward to the wasting time interval; thus, the effort and the focus required for the difficult task would be far less than what you had anticipated.

Student: You know I always end up hating myself when I do not work with focus and feel like a total loser.

Teacher: The sad thing is when we waste time, we make ourselves feel guilty, which makes us end up wasting even more time because we now need medicine to overcome that guilt. If the world could be changed by being critical, we wouldn't need tools and tactics that actually worked. We would instead be criticizing each other and ourselves 24/7 and getting better at work and life!

When we waste time, we make ourselves feel guilty, which makes us waste even more time!

Student: The world does not change by being critical. Most of us are nevertheless critical of each other and ourselves 24/7.

Teacher: The difference between successful people and the self-critical ones is that the successful ones manage what they could be doing better by taking better actions, instead of playing the game of guilt.

Student: The guilt game is something I have already played, and it has brought zero positive results.

Time to experiment with what successful people do.
Guilt will never bring out the best in me, no?

Teacher (smiling): The teacher has appeared!

How Do I Deal with Criticism?

Student: No matter how strong or better I get, I often find myself struggling to deal with criticism.

Teacher: Where do you get the most criticism from?

Student: Sometimes online, from random people.
Most often offline, from people who are not at all random.

Teacher: I have a simple life rule – If I do not take someone's advice seriously, then I will also not take their criticism seriously.

Student: Wow. And how do you decide whose advice is not to be taken seriously?

Teacher: We all know that differentiation innately.

Would you take life advice from a troll seriously?

Student: Never.
Because I don't know if they really mean it or if they are really mean.

Teacher: Exactly. That is what helps us put things in perspective.
Their criticism is not about you. Their criticism is a reflection of their unhappiness in their own life.
They are just using you as an outlet to vent their emotions.

Student: If true, that is really tragic.

Teacher: It is. All of a sudden it makes you have empathy towards them, instead of anger!
Which is the most liberating emotion to have.
Otherwise, we are simply puppets letting the advice of people who have zero context cloud the context of our life completely.

Is that what you had signed up for, my friend?

Student: It almost makes me pity myself, for taking them seriously in the past.

Teacher: Now let's look at the criticism from people who are not random.

Student: Yes – family, friends, colleagues, managers. Acting as trolls.

Teacher: But they are criticizing you free of cost, to make you a better person!
Why does it hurt?

Student: Some of them I love a lot.
With others, I have a love–hate relationship.
The ones I love, I wonder why they criticize me.
The ones I don't love as much, I ask the same question.

Teacher: What is making you run away from people who have good intentions towards you?

Student: I can't pinpoint it exactly.
But I want to feel safe around them.
Criticism does exactly the opposite.

Teacher: In our academics, we pass one grade,
and then move to the next.
The next grade is more difficult, but this is
because we are now at a place where we are
able to deal with the difficulty level.

Student: I never thought of it that way! Can
you explain it a bit more?
Teacher: Criticism from our loved ones hurts
us because we have put them on a pedestal.
However, true love also means showing the
mirror.
Only when we separate the message from the
messenger will we be able to truly reflect on
what they are trying to tell us.
There is a line by Anthony De Mello that says:
'Examine what is said, not who speaks.'

Student: That makes so much sense now!

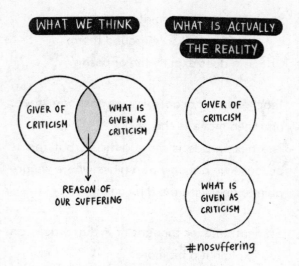

'Examine what is said, not who speaks.'

Teacher: All things seem to get better when we look within.

Student: But why do they criticize us in the first place?

Teacher: Where you are coming from is a place where you do not want to appear 'bad' in the eyes of someone close to you.

Where they are coming from is a place where they don't want you to appear 'bad' in the eyes of the rest of the world.

Student: You are telling me that they are trying to help?

Teacher: Only if you ask yourself the question 'What is it that they are trying to tell me?' instead of 'Why are they after my life?'

Student: Hmmm. Separate the message from the messenger.

Teacher: Absolutely.

And you always have a choice to accept it or not.

If you accept the criticism as something to work upon, you will almost always find yourself in a better spot than you were before you got that feedback (and chose to label it as criticism).

Student: Does that mean feedback is always a choice?

Teacher: Even in our darkest moments, when we think we don't have a choice, we always have a choice.

Student: I will only know of this when I start experimenting with what you said.

Teacher: Which is the right way to go about it.
Do not believe anything I say.
Experiment.
The moment any of this validates your life experience, nothing else will be able to shake the truth that you have just discovered for yourself.

Student: I will, I promise. But I still have a question.

Teacher: Please go on.

Student: Why does negative criticism from parents still hurt?

Especially about the life choices we have made after a lot of thought?

Teacher: Because they are the first people we looked up to.
But the mistake we make is to take their opinion as criticism.

Student: It is easier said than done.

Teacher: If it was easy, it wouldn't need to be said.
This brings me to the part about their opinions that most of us mistake for criticism.

'My parents think I should become an engineer. My parents do not want me to switch careers.'
That is simply their opinion. They disagree with your opinion. But they are not critical of who you are as a person.

In which case, it becomes your responsibility to give their opinions the same objectivity as

'What is their opinion trying to tell me?'

Student: Which is? To me their opinion comes as imposing and dominating.

Teacher: Your parents grew up in a very different world. Where survival was key and only a few limited life choices had a high probability of ensuring that survival.

They aren't imposing, they are concerned. Which does not stem from their lack of acceptance of you, but rather from a lack of awareness of the opportunities you are blessed to explore.

Student: So how do I educate them about my world?

Teacher: Just like they educated you on what the world looks like.
One step at a time.
One conversation at a time.
Clearing one doubt (with patience) at a time.

Student: Does this hold true when I am criticized by my manager or my colleagues as well?

Teacher: Why would it be any different? No one rises every morning wanting to mess up your life.
If they say something, it must have a reason. Find that reason. It is your responsibility to do so.
If you think of it as criticism, just because you felt bad about it or thought it was unfair, guess what?
You are still where you were.
Nothing has changed. Nothing has moved.

Student: It seems to me that life is all about building more self-awareness.

Once I know what drives my emotions, I somehow understand how to manage them, is it?

Teacher (smiling): The teacher has appeared!

How Do I Build a Habit of Reading?

Student: How can I build a habit of reading? I have tried it multiple times, but failed almost every time!

Teacher: What is the problem you face?

Student: I pick up a book. Start reading. And then sooner or later, I end up putting the book down and get back to wasting my time scrolling.

Teacher: I hear you. Tell me something, how do you pick the books you want to read?

Student: Author recommendations on Twitter, newsletters or sometimes I chance across them on a friend's Instagram story.

Teacher: A big mistake most people make while starting their reading journey is to pick a book that will make them look smart in front of others.

Student: Yes, of course. But why is that a mistake?

Teacher: Because the books that contain depth are the ones that assume that the reader is already comfortable with reading. However, most of us don't have the habit of reading for pleasure. We haven't picked up a single book beyond the ones we had to read at school and college. Our patience to absorb the 'non-academic' wisdom at this point is at a low level.

Student: This point hit home.
I want to look cool but haven't read a book beyond my academic ones.

Teacher: Which is why an effective way to begin your reading journey is to start from scratch.

Student: What is the meaning of starting from scratch here? Don't I already know how to read?

Teacher: You do. Starting from scratch means starting with the books that YOU are excited to read.

What do you think would make you excited about reading?

Student: I loved comics as a kid!
But now I can't read them, I'll look foolish :(

Teacher: The reason most of us do not end up getting wiser is that we worry about looking foolish in front of people who are not even thinking of us!

Student: That's a sad realization.

Teacher: And a much-needed one.
If you loved comics as a kid, that is where you should reignite your love for reading

again. Start with reading comics so that you look forward to the process of reading and getting lost in that world, instead of getting distracted by the outer world.

Student: Did you also start your reading habit like this?

Teacher: Exactly like this.
As a kid, I started with the standard *Tinkle*, *Chacha Chaudhary*, *Pinki*, *Billu*, *Nagraj* and *Super Commando Dhruv*. With time, I moved on to *Asterix* and *Archies* comics.
After devouring them for almost my entire school life and feeling comfortable with the process of reading, I moved on to fiction and non-fiction, the kind of stuff I continue to read to date.

Student: Oh, you are such a voracious reader, I thought you started with these intellectual kinds of books from the start.

Teacher: Even a Mercedes sports car starts at zero to reach Formula1 speed!

Student: But won't consuming comic books be purely entertainment? What will I gain from it?

Teacher: Every small habit has multiple repercussions.

Suppose you have nothing to do over a weekend, so you decide to stay glued to your couch and watch Netflix 6–7 hours straight.

But do you know what other repercussions that entertainment brings?

Over a period of time, prolonged sitting makes you obese, screen time affects your eyesight, numbing your senses and your mind; you tend to eat more, and your bones forget what it is to stay active.

In the case of reading comics, entertainment brings about a habit of reading, an understanding of human behaviour, an ability to stick to a story of resilience, distance yourself from screen time and, most importantly, move towards your next level of reading – the intellectual books that you want to read.

Student: But I had another question – can I not get this wisdom just by watching videos and why do I have to consume good content only by reading?

Teacher: I like your question.
Here is what reading does: When you read, you use your visual sense.
During this process, you cannot do anything else – write, speak, listen, anything – because everything is now a distraction taking you away from reading.

When you watch a video, on the other hand, you'll have suggestions of other videos, you will be required to double tap, and the entire experience is designed to keep you more captivated instead of allowing you to focus.

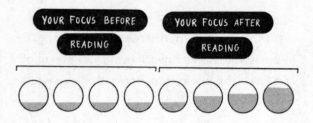

Student: I know, I can vouch for that!

Teacher: That is why the entire exercise of reading without any external stimuli is the most beautiful way of keeping yourself focused.

This process then ensures that whatever you consume, whether it is videos, podcasts or audiobooks, becomes an act of engagement. You have little chance of getting there without building a habit of reading.

Reading replaces mindless entertainment with learning and eventually leads to enlightenment.

Student: So when I start reading the books I wish to read, how should I read them? Is there a goal I should be chasing?

Teacher: Ideally none. But if there is one goal, let it not be the number of books you have read.

The world has millions of books, and it is impossible to read all of them.

So the race should not be to read as many of them as possible.

The race should be to absorb as much from them as possible.

I, for instance, read every day for 30 minutes. It doesn't matter if that means 10 pages or 30 or if it translates into 10 books a year or 50! I love my 30 minutes of reading every day.

For a deep book, I read slowly. For a book that's easy, I may end up reading a lot.

Do not force a target on yourself.

Student: So start by reading books that you wish to read instead of books that you think will make you look smart. Read for a stipulated time every day and over time you will build the habit of reading.
Right?

Teacher (smiling): The teacher has appeared!

How Do I Build Meditation into My Lifestyle?

Student: I want to start meditating. I have to find a way of controlling my emotions.

Teacher: Meditation does not make you control your emotions.
It instead makes you aware of them.

Student: But then what's the point of meditation?

Teacher: Imagine standing on the side of a road.
You see different cars going by – white, red, black, blue.
You don't do anything. You just observe them.
They come and they go.
But you stay still.
Watching them.

Those cars are the thoughts in your mind.

Meditation does not make you control your emotions. It makes you aware of them.

When those cars pass by, you do not board them, control them, or stop them. You do nothing. You merely observe them.

That is what you do in meditation.
You don't get married to your emotions.
You simply observe them.

Student: Honestly, at this point, I don't have the time for this. I need a pill to control my emotions.

Teacher: Have you tried meditation?

Student: I tried it once for two days when we were taught meditation in college. But because I did not get any results, I stopped doing it!

Teacher: Did you think you would change 20 years of conditioning in two days?

Student: I realized I couldn't. That is why I stopped it.

Teacher: Then that conditioning will only get worse.
And make itself stronger.

Student: So, do I sit in a yogi position for 60 minutes every morning and evening?
I'll get bored!

Teacher: (laughs)

You don't need to do it for 60 minutes every day, my friend.

You can start with as little as 10 minutes every day.
And in about 2 years, you will get to a place of meditating for 30–45 minutes every day.

Student: Whoa! It is good to know that I can start with just 10 minutes.
And what do I do in those 10 minutes?

Teacher: Start with guided meditation. There are enough apps and videos that can help you there.
You will listen to a voice that will guide you through what needs to be done.
Make that voice your North Star.
Follow it, assuming it knows the truth.
The voice will encourage you to focus on your breath and observe yourself.
That itch, your heartbeat, the sound outside.
It will be hard to steady your mind early on, but with each passing day, you will get better at it.

Student: And what is the eventual help that meditation will offer?
What does it actually do to oneself?

Teacher: It calms you down.
It allows you to experience your emotions vividly.
You will actually know when you are getting angry, when you are happy, when you are nervous, when you are surprised.
Because you would have spent time observing yourself as someone external to you would.

WHAT MEDITATION REALLY IS

Am I supposed to stay in the moment, or let it go?

Stay in the moment as you let it go.

Student: You said that when I am being a witness to my emotions, I do not respond to them; I just observe them and let them go.

However, the truth is, I don't want to let a few things go.

If someone was mean to me, and I can see the anger cropping up within myself because of them, I do want to speak up against that behaviour.

I will be a nice person and not seek revenge from them. But I do not want to suppress my emotions.

Teacher: Suppression and being a witness to your emotions are two entirely different things.

Suppression is feeling those emotions actively but not doing anything about them or doing something and regretting it.

Neither of these is the right tool to deal with negative emotions.

The only way to deal with them is to be intensely aware of your emotions.

Which is what meditation teaches you.

Once you observe your emotions, there will be two directions you may want to take:

a. You will realize that an action or reaction is not warranted. Or,

b. Your action will be thought out and not impulsive.

Student: But if I have gotten to a place of witnessing my emotions and I can also see the benefits of that trickling down into my life, does that emotion still live within me?

If yes, how is meditation helping me?

Teacher: That's an honest question.

The sheer awareness of an emotion makes you get rid of that emotion. Because the purpose of the emotion is not to solve what you are feeling but to make you aware of what you are feeling.

If you are feeling the emotion of jealousy, its purpose is to make you aware of the inadequacy you are feeling in your own life.

If you are feeling the emotion of anger, its purpose is to make you aware of an unfulfilled need within yourself.

The minute you observe the emotion and realize the reason behind it, the emotion disappears. Because its purpose has been served.

It is such a miraculous thing.

Student: How do I know when is the right time to pick up meditation?
Honestly, it is only during distress that I think I must pick up meditation.

Teacher: The best time to plant the tree was yesterday. The next best time is today.
The right time will be when you begin to meditate, and you will know that it's working for you.

Student: I understand. I almost expected this answer.

Teacher (smiling): The teacher has appeared!

PART 2

MANAGING YOUR CAREER

How Do I Build Trust?

Student: I secretly envy people who are trusted by everyone.

Teacher: Why do you envy them?

Student: Because I'm not able to get people to trust me as much.

Teacher: What's stopping you, my friend?

Student: By now I know the answer is – I am the one stopping myself.
But I don't know how to build trust for myself in others.

Teacher: It is beautiful that you recognize the importance of trust.
Most people think that it is not important to be trusted.
Hard work and intelligence can compensate for that.

Let me tell you a story about another student just like you.

She had just started her job at a consulting firm right after graduating from a top B-school.
She was from a science background. And at B-school her most dreaded subject was accounting. She hated it!

Guess what her first assignment was upon joining the firm?

Student: Oh no! Accounting?

Teacher: Guess how well she did that job?

Being smart and witty can never compensate for lack of trust. Ever.

Student: Not well, I suppose.

Teacher: Every single day, she did a mediocre job on the project and submitted it to her manager. The manager would point out errors in it and she would immaculately fix the errors.
But the same thing kept repeating.

Student: Isn't that great?
The manager is taking care of the student's mistakes?

Teacher: It is anything but great.
Because the job of your manager is not to correct the mistakes in your work.
The job of your manager is to build upon your work.
If they are correcting your mistakes, they are doing your job.
Or in other words, by committing the mistakes repeatedly, you are not allowing them to do their job.

Student: Oh. So how did your student's manager handle it?

Teacher: The manager let things be for a couple of weeks. And when things didn't change, the manager set up a 1:1 with my student.

Which is when the manager said the truest words about trust:

'When you submitted your first work, I reviewed it since it was the first time. And it had errors. I pointed them out to you, and you fixed them wonderfully.

But the next time you sent another piece, it had errors too.

You did fix the errors again, but now I do not know if the work you submit is error-free or not.

I know the end result is error-free, but I still have to check the first version of your work to check if there are any errors.

You see how that is not good use of anyone's time?

I have gotten to a point where I unfortunately don't trust you.
And, *if I can't trust you, it doesn't matter how smart you are.*'

Student: I never saw it this way. Wow!
So the way to build trust is to do error-free work?

Teacher: Seth Godin, who is one of my favourite thinkers, has a beautiful definition of trust: Trust isn't about 'nothing will ever go wrong'.

Instead, trust is that even when things go wrong, you know that everything that was needed to be done to prevent it was done and everything needed to fix it will be done.

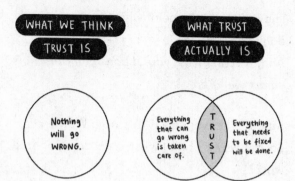

WHAT WE THINK TRUST IS

Nothing will go WRONG.

WHAT TRUST ACTUALLY IS

Everything that can go wrong is taken care of.

TRUST

Everything that needs to be fixed will be done.

Student: That is so deep.

So building trust has multiple dimensions to it?

Teacher: Building trust is a function of three things:

One, to be there for people when times are difficult.

To be there for your friend when they are not at their best.

To be there for your manager when everyone else in the team is moving on.

To be there for your loved ones when they are not in a place of giving love but are needing it.

To be there when it is easiest to move on, yet you choose to stay is when trust is built.

Student: Isn't this the hardest thing to do?

Teacher: Which is precisely the reason there are very few people whom we can trust.
It is easy to be there when everything is going well.
It is intensely hard to be there when you don't need to, perhaps don't even want to, but you know you should be there.
It brings me to the second core ingredient of building trust.

Being accountable for what you do.

Student: I am not sure I fully understand.

Teacher: Long ago, there was a sculptor who lived on top of a mountain. He was working on making the best statue in the world.
He wished for it to be so spectacular that people from villages all across the valley would marvel at it.

The sculptor worked on it for several months. When he was done, he invited a friend to have a look at it.

The friend absolutely loved it!
However, the nose of the sculpture was slightly chipped. 'I have never seen such a beautiful statue in my life. The nose is slightly chipped, but that's okay. People standing many feet below won't even realize it!'

The sculptor took his axe and broke the sculpture!

Student: Was he mad? Why did he do that?

Teacher: 'It doesn't matter whether the world can see it or not. It is enough that I have seen it. I define my own standard,' said the sculptor.

Student: That is such a strong definition of accountability.

Teacher: When you are accountable to yourself, it doesn't matter who else you are accountable to.
Because you speak your truth, it doesn't matter who else sees it – because all they would see is the truth.

Student: Defining your own standards. Makes sense. And what's the third ingredient to building trust?

Teacher: The third ingredient of building trust is sticking to your commitments.
You do what you are supposed to do without having to provide a status update.

Student: But people are always asking for a status update. Even before the deadline.

Teacher: Why do you think that is the case?

Student: I don't know. Because they are not sure if it will actually be delivered on time?

Teacher: Precisely.

Maybe their past experiences have shaped their current realities.

Or maybe the lack of communication from your side has made them uncomfortable.

Either way, place yourself in the shoes of the person and share proactive updates. Not when asked for it. Instead, regularly, without being asked.

And if for any reason you are unable to deliver on your commitments, request for more time. Much in advance.

Student: Fantastic. This is so clear.

Be there in difficult times.

Be accountable to yourself.

Stand by your commitment.

Because it doesn't matter how smart I am if people cannot trust me.

Teacher (smiling): The teacher has appeared!

How Do I Find My Passion?

Student: This is something that bothers me often. I am an adult. I have a job. I pay my bills. But I am not driven by what I do. I don't think I have found my passion.

Teacher: The truth about passion, my friend, is that it is not something that is found at a particular place at a particular time.
Your passion isn't lying somewhere, waiting to be found.
You grow it by pursuing things that interest you, and over time, an amalgamation of all of those becomes your passion.

Student: But I am already 23 and should be settled by now.

Teacher: Everyone in their 20s thinks they are too old.

And they are in a hurry to find their passion and settle down.
Because everyone tells you to settle down.
Finish your education, get a job, get married and settle down.

Here is an alternative way of looking at your passion.
Spend your 20s exploring your passion.
Spend your 30s honing your passion.
Spend the rest of your life reaping the benefits of your passion.

No one should settle down. Keep up that fire. Keep moving the needle. You weren't born to just settle down!

Student: That sounds like a lovely plan on paper. But how do I execute it?

Teacher: Heard of the word ikigai?

Student: Sounds familiar. It's the name of a famous book, isn't it?

Teacher: Well, the book is written on this famous concept of ikigai. In Japan, there is an island called Okinawa. A highly unusual percentage of seniors on Japan's Okinawa Island live to the age of 100 years and beyond. Their secret, they claim, is 'ikigai'.

Student: And what does that mean?

Teacher: Ikigai is a Japanese word. It doesn't have a direct English translation, but loosely translated, it means 'the reason for being', or 'the purpose of one's life'.

Student: Passion?

Teacher: Or passion, if you wish to think of it that way. It is a simple yet powerful concept. It was only after I read and understood the concept of ikigai did I realize that I had been unknowingly applying its principles all throughout my life.

All of my seemingly random decisions in life, which made no sense in my 20s, suddenly made sense when viewed through the lens of ikigai.

Student: Tell me more, please.

Teacher: Ikigai starts with a fundamental question, 'What is it that you love doing?'
We all love doing something.
For some it could be singing, for some working with numbers, for some connecting with people, for some food.
Unfortunately for most, what we love doing is crushed along the way and replaced by 'what the world expects us to do'.
And hence we become engineers, CAs, lawyers and doctors.

Not because that is what we love.
But because that is what we are told we should do.

Student: You are beginning to share my story now.

Teacher: This is everyone's story, if it's any comfort.
Start with this question: 'What do I love doing?'
And make a list of all possible things.
Do not stop at just your assessment of it.
Ask your family: What are the things I used to love doing as a kid?
Ask your friends: What are the things you see me doing that make me look happy?
Ask your colleagues: What are the things that make me jump with joy when I have to do them?
Investigate.
Make a list as long as you can.
Somewhere in there lies your ikigai, your search for your passion.

Remember – you won't find it.
You will realize it.

Student: I love this already.
Let's say I have this list. What next?

Teacher: Of all the things you love, you may not be good at all of them.
I love singing.
But to the world's benefit, I sing only behind closed doors.
So of the things you love, which are the ones you are good at?

Student: Hmmm. Interesting. What will be the definition of good here?

Teacher: That is a good question.
The answer lies within.
You may find yourself good at something already.
Or you may sense the potential of becoming good at something.

Student: If this is my own assessment, could it not be false?

Teacher: Potentially. Hence I would also recommend asking the same people you used to prepare the list of all that you love.
Ask your family, friends, colleagues what are the things that you are good at.

Student: So things that I love and things that I am good at. I can see where this is headed. Is that my ikigai?

Teacher: Want to know the truth?
This isn't your ikigai.
But this is your passion.

Student: Sorry, what? I thought ikigai was my passion.

Teacher: Recall that the loose meaning of ikigai is the reason for being. Your true reason to exist.

According to ikigai, things that you love and are good at comprise your passion. But they are still incomplete when it comes to defining the true purpose of your being. There are 2 missing elements still.

Student: Which are?

Teacher: Number 3 is: 'Is it something that the world needs?'
Of the things that you love doing and are good at, not everything will be something that the world needs or cares about.

Student: But how do I know whether something is needed by the world or not?

Teacher: Just as for the other elements, this definition too is personal.
You define the need and its importance. Imagine working in a job that you love and are good at, but every day you feel as if the world doesn't really need this job to exist.

You lack meaning, a sense of purpose.
It nags you, but you never truly understand why.

Student: I know this feeling. This precise feeling. But I could never explain it.

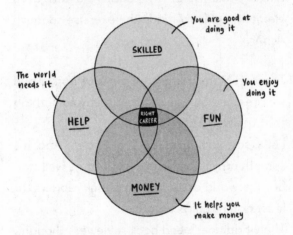

WHAT A RIGHT CAREER LOOKS LIKE

SKILLED — You are good at doing it

HELP — The world needs it

FUN — You enjoy doing it

RIGHT CAREER

MONEY — It helps you make money

Teacher: We have all been there.
In the same breath, there may be a comedian, or a singer, or an artist who is great at what they do, love what they do and genuinely

believe that they help the world by sharing their art with the world.

As I said, this is a personal choice, a personal definition of meaning that you attach to the things you truly love and are good at.

Student: This is deep.

While we were going through ikigai, I was making this list in my head. And this third element suddenly made the exercise so much richer.

Teacher: Many things that make us happy and we are good at may not be directly something that the world needs.

Let's say you love reading books. And it's something you are really good at as well.

But the world does not need book readers, at least not in a direct manner.

The world does need book reviewers though.

Or people who curate books on a particular subject.

Or people who create notes from books and share them as summaries.

In essence, there will be work that is required to translate what makes you happy and what you love doing into something the world needs.

Student: I understand. What did you do?

Teacher: My ikigai today is teaching.
It was something I always loved from childhood.
And it is something I have become good at over the years.
I had to convert my love for teaching into something that the world needed.
Which is where I put in my time, my patience and my efforts.

Student: Super clear now. Thank you.

Teacher: Which brings us to the last element.
In my opinion, the easiest one is once you have figured out the first three.
'Does it make me money?'

Student: Haha. You call it the easiest? Isn't this the hardest?

Teacher: I call it the easiest once you have figured out the first three.
Because in my experience, money becomes a natural by-product over time once the first three are figured out.
It takes time though.

Student: And is that why you stated that 20s is the age for exploration? What you meant is your 20s is the time you spend finding your ikigai.

Teacher: Correction.
Your 20s is the time you spend on building your ikigai.
Or, for that matter, whenever you start.
If you start in your 30s, in your 40s or even beyond, do not expect it to pop up one day.
It is a journey you will have to undertake.
Perhaps the most fruitful journey of all.

Student: This was wonderful.

What makes me happy?

What am I good at?

What does the world need?

How can I make money from it?

If I find these 4 things, the intersection of them is my ikigai.

Even though I haven't found it yet, simply being aware of this gives me strength.

Teacher (smiling): The teacher has appeared!

How Do I Pick the Right Career?

Student: I am now aware of ikigai as a means of exploring my passion. Does this apply to your career as well?

Teacher: Do you think your career and your passion are disconnected?

Student: Not really. But how do I find my ideal career, if I am already in another career?

Teacher: At first, you have to know that the job you currently have pays your bills.
Don't dismiss that job.
It provides for something critical – financial stability.
At the same time, don't make it the centre of your existence.
Use it for your survival and then with whatever time is left, you use it to explore your dream career.

Student: So I do not have to be the best in the world at my job if I don't intend to continue to do it for the rest of my life?

Teacher: For this job, yes. This does not mean you are not going to do your job. But you are certainly not going to go beyond your job.

An important thing to note is that you are not going to compare yourself to anyone.
A 19-year-old making a million dollars; people making it to the top companies straight out of graduation; someone your age making 2X money of what you make – all of these are distractions.
No matter how true they are, they are not your life.
They are someone else's life.

If comparison led you to where you wanted to go, people would do nothing other than compare.

What you want from your life is what you will chase.

It may be the same thing as them.

And that's fine too.

However, you will get what you want in your life when you take the actions in your life, not when you compare your life to someone else's and take no action because your heart is filled with envy instead of encouragement.

Student: Envy comes instantly every time I see someone else with something that I was chasing.

How can I get rid of that?

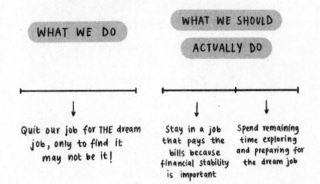

PICKING THE RIGHT CAREER

WHAT WE DO

WHAT WE SHOULD ACTUALLY DO

Quit our job for THE dream job, only to find it may not be it!

Stay in a job that pays the bills because financial stability is important

Spend remaining time exploring and preparing for the dream job

Teacher: By taking action towards what you want.

And by continuously reminding yourself that you are here to live your own life and, no matter how different it is from that of others, that is the only thing that will fulfil you.

Envy empties. Action achieves.

Student: I have only my life to live. Thank you for the reminder!

Teacher (smiling): The teacher has appeared!

How Do I Change My Career?

Student: I am at a place in my career where I don't feel 'at home' about it any more.
I thought this was the career for me but I am not happy with it.

Teacher: How old were you when you picked up your current career?

Student: I was 16, after having completed tenth grade. Not too young, I assume!

Teacher: At what age did you get your driving licence?

Student: At 18, because you cannot get one before becoming an adult.

Teacher: Weird, no? We have to decide our careers before we are even eligible to drive a vehicle. Do you think people know how to do that?

Student: I didn't know back then. Today I know my current career is not for me. But I don't see a way out. I am already several years into it.

Teacher: Before you consider changing your career, it is critical to acknowledge the importance of financial stability.

Student: My family and friends also say that, insisting I shouldn't switch careers.

Teacher: I'd argue that financial stability is important to switch your career.
Switching your career is not going to be easy. It will take time.
Which means you do not want to put the pressure of making money on it from Day 1.

Student: But how will I switch my career if I continue in the same job with the financial stability it brings?

Teacher: Do your job well, so that it pays your bills.

And the rest of the time – your nights, your weekends, your holidays – you explore the other careers that interest you.

Your job now is not to win the 'Employee of the Month' award or to become the apple of your manager's eye.

Your job is to do your work diligently and to squeeze out the rest of the time for yourself.

Student: But I feel tired at the end of the day after I have done my job.

I just do not have the time to work on the side!

Teacher: Well, then, continue to be where you are. You will thus be miserable AND tired.

Student: Please do not make fun of me! I am genuinely stuck!

Teacher: If your house was on fire and you were inside the house, would you still cry out aloud that you are stuck and do not know what to do?

No! You will do everything possible to save yourself.

It's tragic we don't act this way when our life and career are on fire.

Student: I understand that it is important to take action.

But some jobs do suck time and energy completely!

Teacher: The key, then, is to become smart about your work, to find smarter ways of doing the same job better, faster, cheaper.

To structure yourself in a manner that you can take breaks so that you get time for yourself.

And to genuinely work hard.

Because you are trying to help yourself. No one else will.

Student: That is work on my part. I understand that.

What if, in my current job, my manager has already given me feedback to buckle up? What if I am not performing well in my current job?

Teacher: You cannot escape being diligent at your work.

You have to do what is required of you and get the job done in a manner that everyone thinks and knows you are good at it.

There is no shortcut to that.

Beyond that, I would ask you to consider not taking on more initiatives.

Remember, this career is not your final destination.

The time you spend here doesn't bring you joy.

So spending more time on it is not the solution.

Student: So what should I be doing when I have the time for myself from my existing job?

Teacher: Set out to explore careers that nudge you towards them, like a traveller with no destination.
With only the intention to become a dedicated student.
One month at a time.
For one area you are interested in.

For example, let's say you want to switch from sales to digital marketing.
For a month, like a student, take up courses in digital marketing.
Speak to people who are digital marketers.
Speak to people who are not digital marketers any more.
Listen and understand both sides of the coin.

At the end of the month, ask yourself honestly: Am I enjoying this? Is it something that I see myself doing?

If the answer is yes, you now dig deeper.
If the answer is no, you pick another career option and repeat.

Student: If I arrive at a yes, what next?

Teacher: Look for opportunities within your own organization.
If not, pick up projects and internships to sharpen your axe.
Engage with online communities and people in similar environments.

At the end of the second month, you again ask yourself: Am I enjoying it?
Based on your yes or no, you go ahead with the same process again.

Student: So I will reach a point where I will either know which career I want to switch to, or I will know the 10–12 areas I do not want to opt for.

Teacher: Yes. The awareness of what not to do is equally important.

Student: Is that not going to take a lot of time?

Teacher: Changing careers will not happen overnight.
It is a place where you will spend most of your waking hours.
It should and would take time.

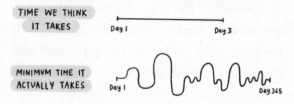

WHAT A CAREER CHANGE LOOKS LIKE

TIME WE THINK IT TAKES
Day 1 ——————— Day 3

MINIMUM TIME IT ACTUALLY TAKES
Day 1 ⌇⌇⌇⌇ Day 365

Student: When I have finally arrived at 'the one', should I consider moving from my existing career?

Teacher: Depends on what the career line is.
If it is another job, then start applying for those jobs.
Send cold emails.
Share your work, your experience.
Reach out to the same communities that you were a part of.

If it is something you wish to do on your own, then start to slowly unlock an income stream from it.
And only once your income from your new career matches your monthly needs, on a predictable basis for at least six months, quit your job.

In a rapidly changing world, the ability to become a student whenever you have to is a superpower!

Student: You know something? As you went through this process I realized that I will have to adopt this process multiple times in my life. The world seems to be changing so rapidly, that I don't know if my next choice of career will be my last one. I doubt it.

Unlike my parents, I might end up having multiple careers. And thus go through this process several times. No?

Teacher (smiling): The teacher has appeared!

How Do I Grow in My Career?

Student: Is growing in your career only about changing jobs or waiting for the yearly appraisals?

Teacher: Growing in your career is always a personal journey.
What looks like career growth for me would not look the same for you, and vice versa.
Thus, we need to start with an awareness of what we want in our career in the first place.

Student: Oh, I want everything.
I want more money.
A nice manager.
Work–life balance.
More growth opportunities.
Bean bags.
Climbing up the corporate ladder.
Perks and privileges.
Free lunch.

A team that lifts each other.
Everything!

Teacher: A sure-shot way to fail in your career is to want everything.

Because it is a substitute word people use when they don't know what is the one thing they want in their career right now.

What you want from your career right now may change over the next 5–7 years, and that's perfectly fine. However, if you do not know the one thing you are chasing right now, you will keep chasing everything but never reach a place of satisfaction.

Student: Who wants to be satisfied in their career? Is it not about going up the ladder?

Teacher: Satisfaction does not mean resting on your laurels and not tasting more success. Satisfaction means feeling happy on your way to the top instead of living in constant anxiety and desire to have more and more.

Student: Will that come only when I know that one thing I want from my career?

Teacher: Look at our parents' generation.
They are an unfortunate example of chasing only one thing irrespective of what it is that they truly wanted. That one thing was stability.
Everything about their careers was about stability.
Most of them still had pretty unfulfilling careers.

Student: Oh, I will always be grateful to my parents for what they did for me and for bringing me up.
But I certainly do not want to have a career like theirs.

Teacher: Stability was the only way they could have ensured survival.
Back then, survival was key.
Money was needed.

Playing the game of corporate ladders was also needed.

Thus, they had to be compliant with the rules of the corporation, whether they liked it or not.

To ensure stability, a lot of them gave up fulfilment and happiness.

Student: I understand.
So how do I know what is the one thing I want right now in my career?

Teacher: That is the awareness you need to build by having a conversation with yourself.
When you are starting out, you may want a lot of money. And that is perfectly fine.
For that, it's okay to work with a boss who isn't super-nice.
To not have a work–life balance.

But because you know that the one thing you want right now is money, you will work with everything, even if it seems unfavourable, with grace and satisfaction.

Student: So all these miseries will still make me happy because I know that my one most important need from the career is getting fulfilled?

Teacher: Exactly.
This is the magic of this self-awareness.

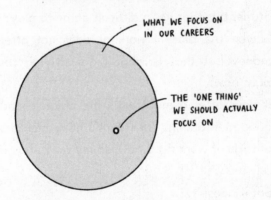

GROWING IN YOUR CAREER

WHAT WE FOCUS ON IN OUR CAREERS

THE 'ONE THING' WE SHOULD ACTUALLY FOCUS ON

Student: But what if after several years of working, I do not want money as much as I want to work with people who challenge me and make me grow?

Teacher: Which is why the second step to growing in your career is to know what would make that happen in the first place.

If you want growth, what makes growth happen?

If you want money, what makes money happen?

If you want a good culture, what is a good culture according to you?

Student: Is that not a difficult game to play? Maybe the place I work at does not offer money but that is what I am striving for right now.

It does offer a great work–life balance and good mentorship, but I think I have mentors outside of work right now, so my work should pay me well.

But it doesn't.

Life becomes difficult again.

Teacher: Life is difficult if you keep proclaiming that it is.

Student: I accept that.

So how do I change things when I know my current job does not serve my current needs?

Teacher: It is about having a conversation with yourself about what a fulfilled need looks like.

If you want a good culture, reach out to friends and seek feedback on how culture operates in their life.

If you want more money, reach out to people whose job offers them exactly that.

If you want good growth, reach out to people who are actually witnessing it in their job!

Student: A first-world problem – what if I do not have friends who have these?

Teacher: Then you leverage the power of social networks, my friend.

People are always willing to help if you show them how.

Student: Help people help me?

Teacher: Absolutely.
By forming connections with them.
By acknowledging the journey they have had,
and by asking them specific questions.

Student: Can you give me an example?

Teacher: Let's say you want to reach out
to someone who works in a company that
apparently pays their employees lavishly,
and you want to work in that or a similar
company. So you reach out to them, stating:

Hey XXX,

I really appreciate the work you have been
doing at XYZ company. The company's
achievements and how your career has grown
are wonderful testaments to that.

XXX, I am planning to switch my job from ABC company to XYZ company and want your help in understanding the upsides as well as the downsides of working in a company like this, in general.

Would you be willing to help me here? I have 3 specific questions to ask, and I won't take more than 10 minutes of your time. And we can do it over email itself, or if you prefer a call.

PS: Here you write something that is unique to them (through their content) and comment on how it that so unique. This is to have their attention and get them to say a yes.

If you don't ask, the answer is always no!

What do you think is going to happen when you reach out to at least 5 people like this every single day?

Student: I am going to copy this template of yours. Thank you.

Teacher: That's okay. I borrowed it from someone else as well. We all rest on the shoulders of others.

Student: So what I understand is that at all points of time in my life I need to be self-aware of the one thing that I need from my career the most. That thing can change, but at that moment if I don't attend to it, I will constantly feel underserved.
This is going to be a tough conversation, but I promise to try.

Teacher (smiling): The teacher has appeared!

How Do I Deal with Office Politics?

Student: I find it really hard to deal with office politics.

Teacher: Help me understand what office politics is.

Student: Office politics means people purposely doing things to make sure you don't win.

Teacher: There are two kinds of office politics and they do exist, unfortunately.
One is encouraged in company cultures, which means the top leader in the company follows the same misaligned principles that are being followed at a micro level in your own department.

If your manager encourages politics and that is aligned to how your top leader also behaves, you do not have a choice, my friend. It is not politics any more, it is the way the company operates.

You cannot help it.

You can attempt to fight it, but it will be an intense fight.

You can attempt to withstand it, but it will suck all of your energy.

Your only job then is to find yourself another job where the leader is working on setting up a company that wants to create a space where people love to come to work.

Student: So that means because I landed in the wrong place I have to bear the brunt of it by looking for another job?

**If your manager indulges in the same politics that the top leader does, that is not politics.
That is the culture.**

Teacher: Who is responsible for your career? Is it someone else?

The choice is between momentary discomfort in finding a new job and working in a toxic environment.
You choose.

Student: That hits hard. But I admit it is the truth.

Teacher: We now come to the second type of office politics.

The reality of corporate culture is that it is defined at multiple levels.

Every team, department, every floor will have a different culture.

If your team thrives on office politics but that is in distinct contrast to how the top leaders present themselves, you now have a moral responsibility to voice your opinion.

Student: But what if I am a fresh entrant into the team?

Or maybe I have been here for a few months and everyone in the team is of the same political vibe. Would I stand a chance of being heard?

Teacher: If the company thrives and voices a positive corporate culture and you see it across other departments as well, you will only be thanked for raising your voice.

Student: I get you.

However, the brutal reality is that I need that job.

What if I get fired?

What if the leader likes the person indulging in politics more than me and they are not able to see what I am experiencing first-hand?

Teacher: Here is a secret: A leader sees and knows everything.

Even when you don't know, they see and know everything. Including what and who in the company or the department is toxic.

If they do not stay in alignment with who they claim themselves to be, they unfortunately fall into the first category we just spoke about.

Student: Which means if I get fired, I know the leader was faking all along. How did it help me though?

Teacher: Go back to the conversation we just had.

The choice is between momentary discomfort in finding a new job and working in a toxic environment.

You choose.

Student: Not a choice I wish to make.

Let's say the leader is not fake and my manager gets fired instead of me.

How will getting someone fired solve the toxic culture?

Teacher: Our intent is not to start with wanting to get someone fired.

Our intent is to have someone look at our situation objectively and solve it.

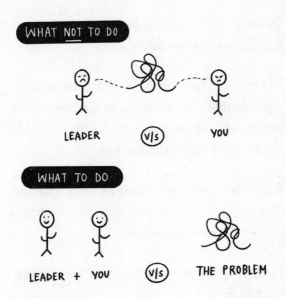

WHAT NOT TO DO

LEADER (v/s) YOU

WHAT TO DO

LEADER + YOU (v/s) THE PROBLEM

You may be wrong in your definition of what is politics, in which case you will end up broadening your perspective.

Or your concern could very well be valid, in which case the company will be grateful that you helped fix it.

Student: If I turn out to be wrong, what will everyone else think of me?

Teacher: That is the unfortunate trap we all fall into – what will others say!

If the culture thrives on objectivity, righteousness and allowing people to be heard, what is the point of wondering about what others would think of you?

Student: I understand that, but I feel scared that even if I make the slightest mistake, people will turn against me.

Teacher: Do you want to know the biggest truth ever?

No one, absolutely no one, would be thinking of you.

We think some people wake up in the morning wanting to screw up our happiness. But no one cares. Everyone is busy thinking about their own lives.

Student: But if I still see myself in conflict with people, how do I get to be at peace with it? I ultimately have to spend most of my day with them.

Teacher: Ask yourself: What do they know that I don't?
Why would they behave so differently from what I would expect them to?
Why would they come up with something that is so dramatically different from what I would come up with if I were in the same situation?

Student: That is a difficult question.

Teacher: Easier than losing your sleep over it. Why are they not treating me well?

Student: How would asking these questions help me, though?

Teacher: We see the world as per the lens we wear.

Even if the world out there is white, a red lens on our eyes will make the world look red.
When we put down our glasses and look at the world through someone else's, we see a different world altogether.

Student: When I see that different world, I have more ideas to ponder over!

Teacher: Yes.
It's possible what felt like office politics before was simply a view through a different lens.

Student: So, if my manager behaves as per how the leadership behaves, I really can't do much about it. I am just in the wrong place and it becomes my choice to either bear it or, as you suggest, look for a different job.
If my manager behaves differently from the standards that the leadership has set, it becomes my moral responsibility to raise the issue. And be ready for the consequences.
And it is possible that what I think is office politics is simply a case of different

worldviews. I need to then ask, what is it that they know that I do not.

That is a lot to consume, but I know what to do now.

Teacher (smiling): The teacher has appeared!

How Can I Be Indispensable at Work?

Student: Is it possible to be indispensable at work? To be so good that not having me on the team is something that scares my manager?

Teacher: Tell me, if you are asked to do something and you do it well, will you be indispensable?

Student: I think, yes. If I do it better than others.

Teacher: Does that mean that once others start getting better than you, you will be dispensable?

Student: Oops. Didn't think that through. Yes, I guess.

Teacher: Being better than others is a constant chasing game. It does give you an extra edge, but it is usually momentary. Because you do not control how good others are.

Student: But if I am doing my work really well and others are doing less than me, is that not enough?

Teacher: That is the biggest mistake most of us believe in – that our job is to get things done. In my opinion, that is never sufficient.

Student: Why so?

Teacher: Because if someone comes along and does the task better, faster, cheaper than you, you are going to be eventually replaced.

Student: Then how do I go about making myself indispensable?

If we just do what we are supposed to do, we will just get what we are supposed to get.
Not what we desire to get.

Teacher: Most of us, when given a task, think about what to do.

That is the output.

And focusing on just the output will make you dispensable or replaceable.

But the most curious people, the ones that are truly indispensable, go beyond the output they have to achieve.

They bring something that I call positive unpredictability to their work.

Student: What does that mean?

Teacher: Most focus on the output.

The indispensable ones focus on the outcome.

'Why am I being given this task? What is the reason I am being given this task in the first place?'

As they ponder over this question, they will bring about far bigger and better results than is possible by any output.

All of which are unpredictable.

Output gets things done.

Outcome achieves the reason why things are needed to get done.

Student: Can you explain this with an example?

Teacher: Let's say your manager asks you to prepare a short presentation before an important client meeting.

A presentation that talks about the business of the client, their recent financial data, news reports, etc.

How would you go about doing it?

Student: Oh, I love presentations.
I will google the company name, start with the latest news reports, access their quarterly presentations and prepare a summary.
Basically, in about 10 slides, give a quick gist of what the client is all about.

Teacher: You made the classic rookie mistake. You didn't ask the questions that indispensable people ask.
'Why am I being given this task?'
'Why is my manager requesting this data?'
'How is it going to be helpful to her?'
What do you think is the answer to these questions?

Student: Umm, the manager wants to show the client that she really understands the business of the client?

Teacher: Great. And why is that important?

Student: Because then the client will trust us as a company?

Teacher: Who exactly will trust your company?

Student: The client.

Teacher: Who is the client?

Student: Oh, you mean the person? The one my manager is meeting.

Teacher: Do you know who that person is?

Student: No.

Teacher: Do you think your manager knows who the person is?

Student: Certainly.

Teacher: Do you think it would have helped if your manager also knew everything there is to know about that person, in addition to knowing everything about the company?

Student: I see where this is going.

Teacher: All you had to do was ask the fundamental question.

'Why am I being asked to do what I am being asked to do?'

Student: Wow. This makes it so clear. Does this apply all of the time?

Teacher: The chances to be positively unpredictable are endless.

We can do so all the time.

This reminds me of an instance where a professor at a B-school asked a question at the end of his course:

List at least 3 things that you have learnt from this course.

Only 6 students out of 120 listed more than 3 things they had learnt in the course.

Everyone else stopped at listing exactly 3 things.

They achieved the output.

Failed in the outcome!

We all suffer from this bias, where we think the definition of success is doing the bare minimum. In reality, it is the opposite.

Student: If it is so simple, then why do most people stick to the conventional route of achieving the output instead of going further towards the outcome?

Teacher: It requires work.

It requires us to pause before a task, get into the shoes of the person who gave it and think about what they would expect from us.

Student: It all boils down to this, doesn't it:
Follow the path of hard work and not comfort.
That is where most answers lie.

Teacher (smiling): The teacher has appeared!

How Should I Spend the First 90 Days of a New Job?

Student: I have been enjoying my new job, but I am not yet able to perform at work!

Teacher: Do you expect a toddler to walk?

Student: Umm, no . . .

Teacher: If it doesn't work, do you shame the child?

Student: No, because it's not expected out of toddlers.

Teacher: If they try to walk, will you appreciate it?

Student: Yes, of course.

Teacher: Do you think you answered your question?

Student: But I want to create an impact.

Teacher: Here is a truth most recruiters won't tell you – when you are new at a job, they don't expect you to create an impact from Day 1.
In fact, all they expect is for you to be a keen observer.

Student: Really?

Teacher: What do you think will happen if you try to create an impact from Day 1?

Student: It will make my manager and the leadership proud of me.

Teacher: What is the probability that you will actually be able to create an impact on Day 1?

Student: The probability is low because I don't know the nitty-gritty of the job yet.

Teacher: What do you think will be your manager's reaction if it doesn't work out?

Student: That I was aiming to touch the stars when I hadn't even learned to walk?

Teacher: What will be the practical implication of that?

Student: My manager won't trust my capabilities and my execution, and perhaps my team won't either.

Teacher: What happens if you are not trusted?

Student: My manager will think multiple times before assigning me a task.
And even if they assign me something, they will always have this thought in their head: 'Will she be able to do it?'

Teacher: Do you think it's still wise to attempt to create an impact early on?

If your manager doesn't trust you, it doesn't matter how smart you are.

Student: But if I don't create an impact, won't my managers think that I am not serious and committed to the job?

Teacher: You are partly right.
Seriousness and commitment have two sides:
A. The inputs you contribute.
B. The output you get.
Where do you think your focus is right now?

Student: On the output, the external impact.

Teacher: Do you think seriousness and commitment can be measured even through the inputs you put in?

Student: Maybe. I don't know.

Teacher: Early on in a new job, your input is just as important as, if not more than, your output.

Input in your new job means what you are doing and how you are showcasing that you are capable of getting a job done. It all boils down to 3 essential ingredients:

1. Understanding the culture: Observing how the system functions. How does the company work? How are decisions made?

2. Listening intently: Listen not with the intent to respond but rather to understand. You are not mute but an active spectator of everything happening around you.

3. Reach out to people: Reach out to the staff within your department and outside of it. Engage with them.

How do they do their job? What makes them good? What makes them not so good? What do they like about their work? What do they not like?

All the 3 tasks done actively are the strengthening inputs that create a far bigger output.

Remember, no one expects you to hit a 6 on the first ball of the match.
However, everyone does expect you to be capable of doing that when the moment arises.

Student: Does patience play an important role here?

Teacher: Where does it not play, my friend? :)

You have two choices when you start a new job.

Option 1: Assume you begin cutting trees on Day 1. And ensure you reach a number every single day. But you know what, the number will only progressively reduce because there was no time and space to sharpen the axe.

Option 2: Spend time sharpening your axe every single day. With patience. And consistency. So that when you do start cutting trees, you do it faster than anyone else.

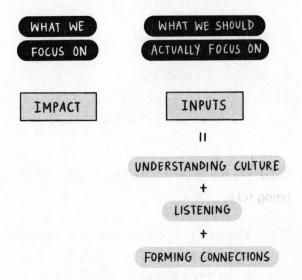

WHAT WE FOCUS ON

WHAT WE SHOULD ACTUALLY FOCUS ON

IMPACT

INPUTS

=

UNDERSTANDING CULTURE

+

LISTENING

+

FORMING CONNECTIONS

Student: I understand the first two points. What I'm not very sure of, though, is how communicating with others amounts to sharpening my axe? To me that seems like something outside of work.

Teacher: Life is very simple.
It has a philosophy most people ignore – if you are nice to people, life becomes easier.

Student: Does this also include people who are fake while being nice?

Teacher: Be nice to people, because you are genuinely nice.
Ask them about their life.
About their experience. Ask what they enjoy and don't enjoy. Where do they come from? What is their family like?

Build meaningful relationships instead of being fake.

When you get to know people at a human level rather than a professional one, they open up like never before.

Now that they have formed a relationship with you, the next time you need their help, they will be more than happy to help you because it's no longer a transactional relationship but one that has transcended those transactions.

Student: That feels so comforting.

However, when I do all the things you mentioned, how would I know the right time to cut the tree with the axe?

Teacher: You wouldn't know exactly when. But at some point, it will be obvious.

Student: As I'll continue sharpening my axe like you said, I won't know when but the moment will arrive to strike.
Are you suggesting that moment is never in the first few days and months of a new job?

Teacher: It could be whenever you are ready for it.
Think of it as the two modes in life.

The first mode is to impatiently, from Day 1, chase an impact.

If an impact is all you chase, without being ready for it, you will always settle for much less than you could have achieved.

The second mode is to be patiently ready to create an impact when the opportunity emerges. It will not emerge on Day 1 itself, but when it does you will create a far bigger impact than those who kept chasing it impatiently from Day 1.

Student: Got it.

Spend time understanding the culture and observing how the system works.

Listen intently. To opinions and reactions around you.

And reach out to people. In your department. And outside of it. Engage with them.

Do all of this with patience, and at the right time you will create a far bigger impact than those who were chasing it from the beginning.

Teacher (smiling): The teacher has appeared!

How Can I Build Multiple Income Streams?

Student: One thing I have always been curious about is how to build multiple income streams. The concept looks so relatable when you see millionaires talking on Instagram, yet so unachievable.

Teacher: Building multiple income streams is like building a building.
The floors are your income streams. But everything starts with the foundation.
In this case, a predictable stable income stream.

Student: Oh, isn't that boring?

Teacher: Imagine what would happen without it.
You will put the pressure on any new income stream to make money from Day 1.

It would be equivalent to training a toddler to compete in the Olympics.
It is not going to happen.

Student: Okay, so my stable income stream will serve as a cushion for me?

Teacher: Yes.
Stick with that income stream.
Be it a job or anything else.
That salary, which most people call a drug, will become your support.
Once you know that you have to continue serving in that income stream, your next task is to take out as much time as possible to devote towards the next income stream.

Student: How do I do that?

Teacher: You build processes.
You outsource administrative tasks of your life.
You set up automation.

All of this with the sole objective of gathering as much time as you can to start exploring different income streams.

You build multiple income streams by first creating a stable predictable income stream.

Student: How do I even know about these income streams? Which ones to pursue and why?

Teacher: Start from the basics and do not overcomplicate.
In my experience, these income streams are almost always a reflection of who you are.
It could mean investing for some or teaching for others. It could be consulting for those who

are good at it or setting up a small business with friends and family.

Student: Am I to understand that while you share the process of building these income streams, the actual choice of the income streams is my personal journey?

Teacher: Always.

Student: I had a question about the process though.
What if I love my job?
Why do I want to do less of it?

Teacher: That is a wonderful question.
I am not asking you to do less of it.
Instead I am making you aware that doing just that isn't going to help you become financially independent.

Something that cost ₹100 in 2012 costs ₹160 in 2022; however, incomes rose from ₹100 in 2012 to merely ₹130 in 2022.

Thus, there was a huge income–expenditure gap as time progressed.

Now, if your job pays you really well, covers more than your expenses and you also enjoy doing it, by all means give as much time as you can to it.
Because the chances of you building more income through that job are way higher than of someone else who does not.

But if your job does not pay you well or you do not see any scope of growth there, a good idea would be to build multiple income streams.

Student: Another question on my mind.
What if I love my job AND I want to build multiple income streams?
Maybe because I do not see myself being just one person?
Is it okay if I go for building multiple income streams despite loving my job?

Teacher: If you love your job and it pays you well, you should still explore.

We have just one life.

Why live it with just one identity?

Maybe you could start by exploring different facets of your personality.

The only thing they would do is add more vibe, energy and success to your current job.

Student: In this case, since it isn't just about making more money, do you still advise me to squeeze out time from my job?

Teacher: Not at all.

The idea is not to make you do less of what makes you happy.

The idea is to make you do more of other things that also make you happy.

Student: Oh wow, that is going to be an awesome ride.

My next question is: How do I take out time

to build these income streams when work is already so demanding?

Teacher: You have to guard your time ferociously. Who else will?
Whatever time you can manage – early mornings, nights, weekends, holidays – you devote that to building a side income.

Maybe you want to write.
Maybe you want to sing.
Maybe your heart colours itself when you paint.
You explore, with the same sincerity as your job. Dedicatedly. Professionally. Consistently.

Three things will come together for you.

1. You would have spent a considerable amount of time exploring and pursuing your interests as if it is a professional stint.

2. You would have done it without the pressure of making money off it (because of your stable predictable income)
3. You would have figured out what feeds your soul and what feeds your pockets. They may not be the same things.

Do you see how wonderful this journey can be?

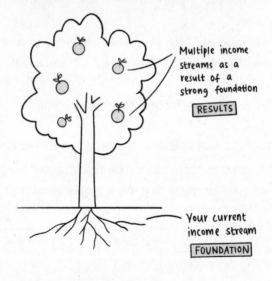

BUILDING MULTIPLE INCOME STREAMS

Multiple income streams as a result of a strong foundation
[RESULTS]

Your current income stream
[FOUNDATION]

Student: Is it really going to result in a big income stream? This process?

Teacher: There is no assurance.
But would you not even try?
And if it does happen, a good thing to always remember is that miracles are simply years of planting seeds until one day fruits are borne.

Student: I loved the core idea of finding a stable predictable income as base so that the pressure of making money is not on your other adventures from Day 1. It almost seems like a philosophy I can extend to other things in life. Am I right?

Teacher (smiling): The teacher has appeared!

How Should I Take a Gap Year?

Student: I see the trend of gap year picking up a lot these days.

What's the right way to take one?

Teacher: Before you do that, it is important to understand why a gap year is important.

In the generations before us, opportunities were limited. There would be 5-6 paths, and people would continue in the same career until retirement.

However, the world is changing and now new opportunities are coming up every 5 years, and the way to keep up with them is by exploring them.

A gap year allows for this exploration.

It is very different from what some of your friends might be doing, which is dropping a year to reattempt an exam they didn't clear.

With changing times, taking time to reflect isn't a luxury. It is a necessity.

A drop year is the opposite of a gap year because it doesn't allow for the most basic ingredient of a gap year – exploring other avenues.

Student: That now seems quite cool. What does the phase of exploration look like during a gap year?

Teacher: There are 3 aspects to a gap year.
1. Becoming a student
2. Building a community
3. Reflecting on yourself
Are you ready to understand all three?

Student: I am.

Teacher: First is to become a student.
Remember that the objective of the gap year is to explore as many different subjects of interest as you can, with the intent to answer 2 questions:

1.   What are the things I can be good at?
2.   What are the things that make me happy?

Start by making a list of ALL the things you wish to explore.
These could be professional things for your career.
Or personal things, focusing on your passion.

Student: Shouldn't the focus of the gap year be on career-related stuff?

Teacher: The goal is to not have such segregation in life at all. Imagine the joy if what you enjoy personally is also what you do professionally.

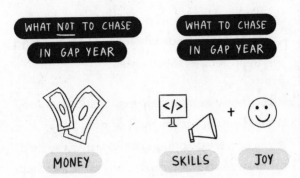

So I would encourage you to not restrict yourself.
Be as exhaustive as you can with the list.

Student: Sure, I understand. What happens once I have the list?

Teacher: Become a student.
Let's say you want to try your hand at software development and you want to see if this is for you or not. Here's how:

1. You pick up courses related to software development and dig deeper.
2. You speak to people who are in the field and understand their perspectives.

3. You also speak to people who were in the field but are not any more to understand their perspective as well.

After that one month of exploration, you will know if you are enjoying it or not.
If you are, we go and dig deeper into the field.
If not, we rinse and repeat with another field that we may want to try our hands at.

Student: How do I dig deeper once I start enjoying the field I pick?

Teacher: You start working on it on your own. Pick a project, intern with someone, work with someone for free, pick up freelancing gigs. Optimize for learning, not for money.

Student: That sounds like a curriculum without exams.

Teacher: You just described life :)
At the end of the year, you will have explored anywhere between 6 and 18 opportunities.

It is incredible how much a gap year with an organized approach can help you uncover.

Student: Indeed.
You mentioned building a community as another aspect. What was that?

Teacher: Just as in school/college, the best learning happens from your peers.
However, a gap year can be a lonely journey.
Especially if your friends did not take one.
You might even doubt your decision and life.
During such a time, it is your peers you will have to rely upon.
So start by finding your peers.

While exploring ideas and fields, find online networks and communities of people, and become a part of them.
To observe, learn and eventually contribute.

Student: Where are these communities?

Teacher: All over the Internet.

Every idea/domain has a community for its most engaged audience.

You may find the design community on Behance or the software development community on Github or the Web3 community on Discord.

That is your homework.

Student: And what role do I play in these communities?

Teacher: The idea is to just be helpful.

Observe. Notice how things work around there. How do people conduct themselves?

Share what you know.

In doing so, you will be led to a place of understanding if you are truly enjoying it.

Remember that this same community will most likely create the next set of opportunities for you.

Student: This already sounds so exciting. And, frankly, liberating. Even comforting. To know that there is a method to the madness.

Teacher: There is.
Which brings me to the last area of a gap area. And the most important one.
Reflection.

Always keep asking yourself these two questions that are the building blocks of a fulfilling life:
1. Am I good at it or can I get good at it?
2. Am I happy doing it?

Student: That sounds so basic; no one will deny it is important. Where do people go wrong in this reflection?

Teacher: Most people take a short-term view while answering these questions.
They think for 6–12 months instead of thinking for 5–10 years.

When one thinks for 6–12 months, one tends to be seduced by short-term joys such as money, status, social validation.

We tend to ignore the fundamentals – fulfilment, joy, contentment.

Student: The pressure of making the gap year work out is perhaps what drives this thinking. You are right, though. If you spend an entire year making decisions only for the next one year, that will be such a waste. Instead, take the year off and use that period to prepare for the next sprint.

Teacher (smiling): The teacher has appeared!

PART 3

MANAGING PEOPLE

How Do I Say No?

Student: Why do I feel so bad saying no? Even though I want to say no with all my heart, 2X of my heart makes me feel bad about saying it.

Teacher: Why do you think it happens?

Student: I don't know! I just feel scared!

Teacher: Let me say something without fully understanding and appreciating the context. You are worried to say no because you care what people may think of you.

The reality is, a lot of us are raised in an environment where saying yes is a reflection of capability and saying no is a reflection of lack of intent.

Student: That is so true! Also, I worry that I would appear selfish or disrespectful to the person making the request.

Teacher: Again, it is about what you think people think of you.

Student: So how do you say no?

Teacher: Here is what I do.
I seek permission to say no.

Student: As in?

Teacher: Let's say you've been invited to a gathering that you do not wish to go to.
Simply because you do not enjoy yourself there.
However, you think that saying no straight away might sound disrespectful.

So you ask: 'Is it okay if I say no?'

How do you think they are going to respond?

Instead of saying no, ask if it's okay to say no? Few will object to that.

Student: I think if it is truly important for me to go, my request would be rejected.
But more often than not, this approach might work.

Teacher: Absolutely.
When you ask this question, you are suddenly asking for permission instead of putting forward your imposition.
And very few people would not grant that to you unless it is absolutely critical for you to say yes.

Student: But why are so many of us so scared of drawing boundaries?
We are scared of saying no in relationships, friendships, offices or anywhere.

How can I change that notion within myself so that I do not feel guilty?

Teacher: There are two parts to this.
One is standing up for yourself.
And two, feeling guilty about it.

Let's start with the first part: Standing up for yourself.

My question to you is:
If something is important to you, why can *you* not give it the importance it deserves?
Why are you so conditioned into thinking that you cannot ask for your space?
When was someone else's space important but not yours?

Student: I don't know.
But all I know is that standing for what is important for me first feels very alien.

Teacher: It's okay to put yourself first.
It's absolutely okay to love yourself first because nothing flows out of an empty cup.

I just wish people would put this as a signboard on their bathroom mirror so that they see it first thing in the morning.

Student: Isn't that selfish?

Teacher: Is there a concept of others in the absence of the self?

Student: That was profound!
But I still feel guilty even thinking of it!

Teacher: Not your fault, my friend.
We have been conditioned into thinking like this.

Did you know that
- most people are not aware of what you are going through?
- they do not perceive the situation the same way that you do?

They need to be helped.
They need to see what we are thinking.
And that happens through a conversation.

Student: So I should be having a conversation with them and letting them know the reason for saying no?

Teacher: Exactly.
Do not expect them to understand.
Explain yourself.

Student: So if I do not want to go to a party with friends, you are saying I can say no while still being respectful to them?

Teacher: Why do you not want to go out with them?

Student: I am tired.
And if I go, I will only bring down the energy of the group.
It is not that I do not love them or their company. But today is just a hard day.

Teacher: Who's stopping you from saying this to your friends?

Student: They might just say I've changed!
It might feel like a rejection to them.

Teacher: If you say no without having a conversation, it might feel like a rejection. However, you need to share what you truly feel with them.

I have been feeling very tired.
I have not been feeling like myself.
I know if I come along, I will not enjoy it, and I may end up spoiling everyone else's mood as well.
So is it okay if I say no?

If they are the right friends, they will understand.
However, if you are not understood, I would argue that they might not be worthy of you, and you are far better off not having friends than having those who want you to not be yourself in a conversation.

Student: This makes it so clear.
So go ahead and ask, huh?
Have that conversation.

And in saying no, there is no shame.
Who knows, it might just help me uncover my
true relationships.

Teacher (smiling): The teacher has appeared!

How Can I Seek Help?

Student: I feel awkward seeking help.

Teacher: As kids, we were rewarded for being intelligent and for knowing all the answers.
That conditioning has transcended into our adulthood, leaving us all feeling ashamed to seek help.
However, seeking help is the most fundamental way of learning.

Student: How is that?

Teacher: Because by seeking help you admit you don't know and are willing to know more.
Not just from people.
Help can come from books, videos, podcasts – virtually anything that can offer guidance in your current context.

Student: Okay, so how do you start seeking help?

Teacher: It all starts with knowing the difference between knowledge and help.

Knowledge is what a Google search can assist you with – how to make a résumé, how to write a business plan, how to apply to a certain college, how to prepare for an interview, etc.

Help, on the other hand, needs to fulfil 4 conditions:

1. You have tried working on the knowledge
2. You haven't entirely succeeded
3. Everything available as knowledge isn't helping
4. So now you have little idea what to do next.

Student: Oh, this is so useful.
I can now predict why help, as per your definition, will actually open up boundaries.

Teacher: True. Because now you have to rely on experience.
Not just knowledge.

Knowledge is the start. The attempt.
Help is not being able to move after the attempt.

Student: But what is the harm in asking for help for the knowledge itself?

When nothing else works, there is always help.

Teacher: Because it suggests that you want it easy.
Help is to elevate your game, not to start your game.
With everything that the Internet has to offer today, you have frankly no excuse for not knowing how to start.
Most people who say they don't know how to start are simply using this as an excuse not to.

The hard work has to be at your end. Asking someone for their experience to help with knowledge is disrespectful of their time.

Student: Why is it so?
Don't they know better than me?

Teacher: Because people will be willing to help you only if you have helped yourself.

Student: So how can I actually get people's help?

Teacher: Let's say you need help with writing a résumé.
To begin with, you do not seek help. You seek knowledge, on your own – résumé formats, common mistakes, dos and don'ts, etc.
You prepare your résumé using this knowledge.
And use the résumé to apply for jobs.
Let's say you get rejected at the résumé stage itself.

You try out a few things using the knowledge available.
But nothing seems to work.
That is when you seek help stating: I applied and got rejected at the résumé stage itself. Made changes and still nothing's happened. I need help!

This shows that you are clear about what you expect and you respect the time and expertise of the person whose help you are seeking.

Student: I am confused between knowledge, help and advice.

I used to write to entrepreneurs seeking help with my business ideas: 'I need your help in fundraising, team building and marketing.'

Teacher: The best is to seek specific help.
When you ask for generic help, you may only get that and no more.
Help that is full of platitudes and lacks insight.

Advice, on the other hand, is what we seek when we have to identify ways of doing something. 'I am confused about whether to choose economics or maths as my core subject. Do you have any advice here?' It rests between knowledge and help.

Do you know the biggest mistake people make while seeking help?

Student: Making it generic?

Teacher: That's close.
The biggest mistake people make while seeking help is seeking advice instead of help or seeking help instead of advice.
When we do so, our needs are not met.

Student: What do you mean?

Teacher: Let's say you are stuck between picking economics and maths as your core subject.

What you need here is advice on picking the right subject.

However, if you reach out to an economics expert stating your areas of interest in the subject, you will get help in understanding economics deeply, instead of advice on the right subject for you. You started asking for help instead of advice.

On the other hand, you know that you are good at economics but not sure about the prospects it can provide for you.

Then asking whether economics vs maths won't give you the right answer.

A better way would be to seek help from an economics expert on your prospects should you take up the subject.

Student: So someone else would be able to help us out only when we know where it is that we need help?

Teacher: You got that absolutely right!
To put it in a model, the best help follows the CAR approach: Context, Action, Results.

What is your Context?
What are the Actions you have taken already?
What were the Results (that perhaps didn't work and hence, you are stuck)?

Knowing this will lead you to the best books, videos and people that can help you.

THINGS TO KNOW BEFORE SEEKING HELP

A- ACTION
What actions
did you take?

C - CONTEXT
What is
your context?

R- RESULT
What are the
results that
didn't work?

CAR APPROACH

Student: That makes things so clear.
And to be respectful of their time, I will make my request in a single line.

Teacher: Not always.

Here are two examples of emails I got yesterday:

'I want to be respectful of your time, so I will keep it short. I am confused about my career and don't know what to do. Please help.'

'I am looking for help to connect me to investors. Attached is my business plan. Let me know your feedback.'

What do you think is the common thread among these two?

Student: They kept it short.
But aren't they too broad? I wouldn't even know how to help them.

Teacher: Exactly.

The best way to get help is to make it easier for people to help you.

Which means you have to deploy empathy for the person you are reaching out to for help. It also means being specific with context, synthesizing it, and figuring out how they can be of help.

Help people see how they can help.

Student: Okay, one more question.

I often start my emails/messages with: 'This isn't worth your time, but I am giving it a shot . . .'

Teacher: No one wants to help those who are apologetic or believe they are not worthy of help.

Do not assume on behalf of others.

Do not undersell your need for help.

Student: Looks like the process of seeking help is a way to stop underselling yourself.

Teacher: If you don't ask, the answer is always no!

Seeking help is one of the most courageous and precious things we can do.

It is an art that, with time, will create the biggest opportunities for you.

Student: I am wondering what I have to offer in return to those who helped me.

Teacher: That is a wonderful thought.

Most people help because it makes them feel good about themselves.

Nothing makes them happier than to know that their help helped someone.

However, they do not hear back from most people they helped.

I would strongly suggest writing to them and letting them know how well you are doing because of the help.

It feeds their desire to help even more, while you complete the cycle of help.

Student: And when you complete the cycle of help you put yourself in a position to help someone one day, right?

Teacher (smiling): The teacher has appeared!

How Do I Convince My Parents About My Career Choice?

Student: I love my parents, and they love me. But we end up arguing all the time, especially about my life choices. How can I build a good relationship with them?

Teacher: Why do you think there is a conflict, if you know they love you?

Student: I really do not know.

Teacher: In my experience, it is because our parents and your generation were born in dramatically different times.

We've talked about this before: the most important thing in our parents' generation was to make ends meet.

To make sure there was food on the table and money to send you to school.

They didn't have that early on as kids, and the only thing they cared about while you were growing up was stability.

Parents seeking stability for your career is not about them going against you.
It is about them being scared of an unstable life.

Happiness, joy were non-existent emotions. All they saw were two sides of life.

One side where someone went to a top college and built a stable career in, say, medicine, engineering, law, CA or a government job. Survival was sorted for such individuals.

The other side was people taking huge risks to become actors, journalists, painters or social workers. Only a handful achieved success or stability through this route.

So they worry because they are still attuned to that world of theirs.

Student: I never looked at it that way.

Teacher: You must understand that while times have changed, our parents haven't.
So we must balance our love and empathy for them with educating them about our life and the choices we make.

Student: How do we do that, though, if we see that our parents have not kept up with the times?

Teacher: Start with yourself first.

Student: Meaning?

Teacher: A good idea would be to convince yourself first that what you want from your life and what your parents want from your life are exactly the same things: peace, happiness, money, success and stability for *you*.

The paths may be different, but the destination is the same.

Student: This is really true.

Teacher: This leads us to another truth about our parents – because their destination is not flawed, it is hard to convince them that their proposed path to that end point might be wrong. This is especially the case since their approach worked really well for them.

Student: And that's the heart of the problem!

Teacher: Which is why we would have to solve it by being very real.

Student: How to do that?

Teacher: What if you start with making them aware of your world?
A lot of what you do and think stems from the content you educate yourself with online, and the people you follow.
What if you start getting them on board into the same world so that their perspective opens up?

Student: But they will resist it and say I am trying to change them.

Teacher: Which is what we don't have to do.
Our intent is not to change them.
But to make them aware of how the world has changed.

Don't start with wanting to convince.
Start with wanting to converse.

Student: Is that all? Making them aware? That sounds too simple, no?

Teacher: There is one more thing. Perhaps the most important.
Let's say one day you decide that you do not want to go for your master's after graduation, and instead want to pursue multiple internships in different fields that you are curious about. How do you think your parents, unaware of your world, will respond?

Student: They will most likely say no :)

Teacher: Which is why you do not have to seek their permission to do it and thereby prove to them that you will succeed.
Rather, seek their permission to fail.

Student: Huh?

Teacher: Remember that scene from the movie *3 Idiots* where the protagonist Farhan does not appear for campus interviews and wants to intern as a photographer instead?

Student: That scene still brings me to tears.

Teacher: The only thing Farhan wanted from his parents was for them to be happy even if he made less money than his friends.
He wanted his abba's permission to 'fail' – to live a life that would make him happy.

Student: I think my parents would say no. This isn't a movie.

Teacher: I think you are underestimating your parents.
But let's assume they do say no.
What if you ask for some time?

If in a parallel world, Farhan's abba in the movie did not agree with his decision to move to photography, what if Farhan had asked for a time of 2 years to try?

If it worked out, great. If it didn't, he would go back to getting a job.

CONVINCING YOUR PARENTS ABOUT
YOUR CAREER CHOICE

I want you to say you'll continue loving me, COME WHAT MAY!

Student: I think Will Smith also did the same by getting into an agreement with his mom to come up with his album.
If the album didn't work out, he would go to college!

Teacher: And he never had to.

Student: All of this seems practical and doable.

We understand that our parents want the same thing from our life that we want from ours, we make our parents aware, we ask them to love us come what may, and we assure them that we will get back to the stable life that they want us to pursue should things go south. The hard work is on us.

We only have to have the courage to take a step to understand them and talk to them.

Teacher (smiling): The teacher has appeared!

How Can I Forgive My Parents?

Student: As a kid, the one thing I would long for was my father's presence.

However, I saw him only in the morning, mostly fighting with mom.

And at the end of the day, returning very late from work, repeating what he did in the morning. He wasn't emotionally there for me.

Teacher: Did you talk to him on the weekends or some few moments here and there on working days?

Student: He was working 7 days a week.

Even if we did talk on some days, it was always about him being happy that I was doing well in school.

So I kept doing well in school, hoping that one day my academic success would mean that he would talk to me about how I was feeling or how my life was shaping up.

There were days I just wanted to beg him to stay home for one day.

He just wasn't there.

Teacher: How is your relationship with him now?

Student: He does take a day off each week now.
He does want me to step out of my room and talk to him.
He now wants those deep conversations.
He wants to mend a relationship that doesn't exist.
But he doesn't want to mend his ways.

Teacher: Why do you think he wants to mend the relationship now?

Student: I don't care any more.
I am tired of caring.
I can love him and respect him but I don't have the capacity to care.

Teacher: It circles back to the same thing for our parents – to them, the only thing they grew up with was a lack of stability.

So they spent their adulthood and a significant part of their life chasing it.

And they rarely stopped to realize that it damaged relationships.

Now that life has become a bit stable, they have the time to reflect on where they could have gone wrong.

However, as adults, their ego comes in their way to apologize, despite knowing that they should.

Student: But how can I go back to the relationship I do not identify with any more?

Teacher: If you didn't identify with it, you would not be talking about it.

Student: My father's sudden interest in me feels alien, though. It feels fake.

Teacher: What if you take the step to make sure it is not alien any more?
I call it 'deemed therapy' for your parents.

What if you write a letter to them seeking forgiveness for all that you did that might have hurt them over the years?

Student: Me seeking forgiveness when I am the victim??

Teacher: You rightly said that.

True love forgives, even when no apology is sought. Because it can.

The beautiful thing about forgiveness is that the moment you seek it, you create a safe space for the other person to also ask for it.

Student: Hmmm. This sounds really hard. I just don't know if I can.

I may end up doing it.

I may not do it either.

I remember how my experiences of being vulnerable as a kid were met with anger.

Teacher: It's absolutely okay to not do this. It's absolutely okay even if you want to do this.

The question is, are you ready for closure?

Student: I am ready for closure.

But if I choose not to seek forgiveness, does this mean I did not try to mend a relationship that could have been fixed?

Teacher: None of this defines who you are as a human being.

Student: So what do I do instead? If not seek forgiveness?

Teacher: I would still suggest talking to them. Love is so infinite that it opens up many doors we didn't think existed.

Approach them not to seek revenge, not to seek an apology, not to prove you were right and they were wrong.

Approach them because you have it in your heart to forgive them.

Student: You mean, do not wait for an apology to forgive?

Teacher (smiling): The teacher has appeared!

How Do I Make Friends?

Student: Isn't it so weird that as a kid I never struggled to make friends and now, as an adult, I find it so hard?

Teacher: You answered the question yourself, my friend!
The best way to make friends is not to start by making friends in the first place.

Student: How is that possible as adults?

Teacher: It is this urge to try to make friends that always makes us present a side of ours that is somewhat fake and pretentious.
Our desperation also prevents us from seeing the other person properly or if there are any red flags in their personality.

The next thing we know, we find ourselves in a friendship that does not have a 'real' version of ourselves, and we feel morally and emotionally obligated to continue that friendship.

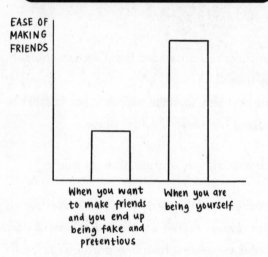

HOW EASY IT IS TO MAKE FRIENDS

EASE OF MAKING FRIENDS

When you want to make friends and you end up being fake and pretentious

When you are being yourself

Student: Is that why we continue being in that friendship despite it not working out for us?

Teacher: Yes.
It is possible we have changed.
It is possible we were never who the other person imagined us to be.

Student: So how do we make good friends with the ones we love to hang out with?

To build strong friendships, do not go out desperately looking for friends.

Teacher: Your best friends are the ones you did not even start with the intent of becoming friends with.
You were simply being you.
So were they.
Because both of you let your guard down, you happened to see sides of each other without a façade.
That authenticity led you to an awareness of what you liked or did not like in each other.

When there was significant overlap, you became friends.

Student: So the way to find friends is to be yourself first?

Teacher: For any relationship. Even a romantic one.
Be interested in people. Genuinely interested in people.
Ask them about their life, their interests, their experiences.
Not to become their friend or to get them to like you.
Instead, with a desire to know them.
Authentically.

Be interested in people. Genuinely interested in people.

Student: But what if I have a defined lifestyle? I go to work and back home. I meet a few folks at work.

I have a few friends outside of work.

And that is the circle of people I am constantly surrounded by.

What if I do not go out much. How to make friends then?

Teacher: Stepping out is hardly about stepping out, especially in this digital world.

There are so many examples of people who became friends on Twitter, Discord, Instagram, etc., just by interacting with each other's content.

Even before they knew it, they were friends Without even meeting each other!

Student: The expectation of not wanting to become friends in the first place is important, isn't it?

Teacher: Absolutely. If and when you meet such friends in real life, their bond is so much stronger than most others would have,

because the bond did not start with any expectation!
Some of them may (or may not) turn into friends.
Some may remain just connections.
And that's okay too.

Student: That is such a complete way to put it!
I had a slightly odd question.
There are some people who think they do not need friends.
They are happy in their own company.

Is that normal?

Teacher: Here is the biggest truth of life – the only best friend you will ever have is yourself.

You know who you are.
Your deepest secrets.
Your ability to talk yourself out of or into something.

How your stories have defined your existence more than anyone else's.

There is no bigger joy than finding comfort in your own presence.

However, there is no bigger disservice to yourself when you use your shyness or social awkwardness or your unwillingness to be uncomfortable as a mask to not meet new people.

Student: How do I know the difference between the two?

Teacher: You already know it in your heart.

You just have to be brutally honest with yourself.

If you are honest, you really do not need anyone else.

If you are not, then you are running away from yourself.

Student: But aren't there different shades of grey to life?

Sometimes I feel wonderful in my own company and I truly do not need anyone else. Sometimes my thoughts get the better of me and I want someone to get me back to my senses.

Teacher: If you are at a point in life where you enjoy your own company, cool, continue enjoying it!
If you are at a point in life where you think you need friends around, connect with people.
They might not end up becoming friends, but even hanging out with people tells you so much about who you want and don't want to be.
And that is precious by itself.

I must say that having friends is actually wonderful because they allow you to meet a part of you that isn't a part of you.
They smile at your success.
Lament at your loss.

Even if your friends are different from you (which is true for many of us), the way they see the world differently helps you expand your definition of what the world is.

Student: That is so comforting!

Teacher: That is the magic of authenticity.
Very few people can share those emotions with themselves while being completely honest.
If you can do that to yourself, you are your best friend.
If you want a friend to do that, that is as good as having an honest relationship with yourself.

Student: All friendships boil down to being honest.

Teacher (smiling): The teacher has appeared!

How Can I Find a Life Partner?

Student: Finding a life partner is so stressful. What if we make the wrong choice?

Teacher: You will find a partner when you are not looking for one.

Student: Say that again?

Teacher: You will find a partner when you are not looking for one.

Student: What does that even mean? Sounds like something Naval Ravikant would say! For me, time is running out. I need to find one asap.

Teacher: You are simply forcing yourself to like someone, putting the pressure of a deadline on yourself and, most certainly because of this you are going to compromise on the values that are important to you.

All of this, with 100% certainty, will lead you to ignore red flags, if any, and settle for a person who is not the one you might want to live your life with.

You will find a partner when you are not looking for one.

You can use this route, and it may work for you. But for partnership and love, I am not sure this is the way . . .

Student: So how do I look for someone with whom I can have a lifelong partnership and love?

Teacher: When you are you and happy with who you are. When you aren't looking for someone to 'complete' you because you have totally accepted yourself, not 'waiting' for someone to come and make your life better. It is then that someone will come into your life.

A meeting might translate into friendship.
You will confide in each other.
Share your highs and lows.
And be genuinely happy for each other.
And you may decide to spend your life together over a few years of such conversations.

Student: Why do you say years? Some people decide in weeks!

Teacher: Because liking each other and wanting to grow old together are two very different things.
In the beginning, if we like someone, we tend to like almost everything about them.

But the more we spend time, we begin to see cracks.

As they see ours.

Are those cracks acceptable to you?

Are yours acceptable to them?

Do you make each other happy despite those cracks?

Or do you make each other miserable because you know of those cracks!

Do your values intersect?

These discoveries and realizations take time.

Student: How do you figure out if the values intersect or not?

Teacher: The first convergence you have to find is around money, career, ambition.

You may want different things from life.

If one wants to grow in their career exponentially and the other makes sure to do the minimum to stay afloat in their career, over time, your paths are going to diverge.

Emotionally as well.

So will the equation around money.

To not be married to money is one thing, but to design your life in a way where one wants money to work for them and the other wants to work for money forever are different points of view.

Student: How do we know the other person's points of view?

Teacher: It starts with knowing your own.
What are your values?
What is super important for you and what is negotiable for you?

Only when you know who you truly are can you have a conversation with the other person about what they want from life.

Student: But what if what I want from life changes over time?
We cannot plan our entire life while young.

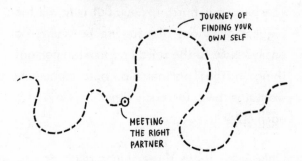

FINDING YOUR PARTNER

JOURNEY OF FINDING YOUR OWN SELF

MEETING THE RIGHT PARTNER

Teacher: Which brings me to the second point of convergence – what you think about life and how it should be led.

What are your principles about life?
And is there alignment around that?
What you do and how do you go about it will change. Why you do things tends to remain constant.
Have a conversation on the WHY.
Why are you the way you are?
What defines your core?

Student: This feels intense!

Teacher: It is hard, I know. But why will the biggest questions of your life be answered easily? Now to the third and most important thing in that partnership: both genuinely want the best for each other and root for each other to succeed.

Only when these three things align do you find the early signs of a relationship that is beyond friendship.

Student: This is difficult.
But the more difficult thing is to find someone in the first place.

Can life partners be found on dating and matrimony apps?

Teacher: Certainly.
With a caveat though: If you are looking for one, you might end up with the wrong one.

Because now there is the 'search' that has to be 'met'.

The longer it takes, the more frustrated you will be, hence the higher the chance of picking the wrong person.

So if you are on these apps, the only reason should be to hang around people on the same wavelength, to see how potentially promising it could be to bump into someone serendipitously.

Student: I have also heard opposites attract. Is it true for love relationships as well?

Teacher: We are always attracted to someone who has something we don't.
The question is, does it create a conflict with who you are, or does it encourage you to become a better version of who you are?

Student: Can partners create conflict for each other?

Teacher: If one side finds it hard to express themselves, does the other side complement them by helping them express themselves or make fun of them?

If one side is outgoing, loud and sociable, and the other is the opposite, do they both ridicule each other for who they are or find a middle ground to understand what each person brings to the table?

Student: Which brings me to another question: Why is it so important to be in a relationship? What if I don't want to get into one?

Teacher: Human life is all about relationships. None of us are islands.

By relationships, it does not only mean love relationships.

You can be in a beautiful relationship with yourself, you can have a wonderful relationship with your family, you can have an absolutely wonderful relationship with your friends.

And if you want to get into a love relationship, it is totally a personal choice.

No one should make you believe you are incomplete and need someone to complete you.
Those who feel complete by themselves make the other person's life better by their presence.
Those who are constantly feeling the need for someone else to complete them transfer that void to the one they enter into a relationship with.

Student: But what if I have the pressure to get into a love relationship?
I do not feel the need to, I feel happy in my company, and more so, I am not ready to get into one.
What should I do then?

Teacher: If anyone asks you to cater to an external deadline imposed due to the 'rules' laid down by society, you would almost always end up in the wrong relationship.

If you are surrounded by someone who makes you believe that, you should always reconsider your relationship with them instead of considering a new relationship forced upon you.

Student: No one can force a relationship on us. Including our own selves.

Teacher (smiling): The teacher has appeared!

How Do I Deal with a Break-up?

Student: I am going through a really bad break-up. I ended a three-year relationship with my boyfriend.
I feel lost. I miss him. I cannot focus.
I am so tired of missing him.

Teacher: What about the break-up do you feel so bad about?

Student: Loneliness.
To know that you were once loved and now you are not.
To come to terms with the fact that the person with whom you were once happy is exactly the one without whom you will have to learn to be happy.

Teacher: I would suggest going through those emotions instead of trying to stop them.

Student: But those emotions make me feel even worse and lonelier.

Teacher: If you do not acknowledge what you are feeling, the suppression will end up making you angry, resentful and underconfident.

Go through those pictures.
Those letters. Those text messages. Those memories.
Those little things that made you smile.
Do not deny yourself this feeling of emptiness.

Student: But I do not want to feel empty.

Teacher: How will you let go of something if you do not even acknowledge its presence in the first place, no matter how scary?

Student: And what will happen if I allow myself the space and time to do that?

Teacher: For many days, it will be the first thing you will think of when you wake up. Until one day, it won't be.

Whatever you are feeling today will eventually fade away.

Student: To be very honest, even though breaking up hurts, the memories of that person are still a solace, to which a deeper part of me wants to cling to.

Teacher: That is the sad and the happy truth of life.
We move on.
Everyone moves on.
We move on with life even when it comes to people who have passed away.

Student: Sounds so scary. Yet so peaceful.

Teacher: It feels scary because we find comfort in the known.
The relationship was known.
The experience was known.

The ups and downs were known.
Suddenly without the relationship, we are in the unknown.
We do not know if we will find someone else.
We do not even know where to look, how to start, what to look for.

The truth is, we were dependent on that relationship to make ourselves happy, instead of being the person responsible for our happiness.

WHAT A BAD BREAK-UP FEELS LIKE

DIFFICULTY LEVEL

BAD

MANAGEABLE

When you wish to get over it and see it as a loss

When you see it as an opportunity to form a relationship with your own self

Student: That hits hard.

Teacher: I do want you to introspect about it deeply.
You can be in a relationship and still be lonely.
Because your sense of love is dependent on someone else telling you that you are loved.

Student: Is this why people want to quickly find another relationship or want that person back, instead of taking some time to build a relationship with themselves?

Teacher: All relationships, when they end, make us feel like we have lost.

However, once the initial phase is over, you will realize that the day you become your own best friend is the day you can pick yourself up despite all odds.
You do not need others' company to make you happy.
You will want a relationship not to be happy but instead to share your happiness with someone else.

Student: However, my break-up has also made me feel guilty.
I broke up with my boyfriend because it was a toxic relationship and I wanted mental peace. However, after the break up, the only things I can remember are the good bits, not the emotional upheavals I went through.

Teacher: A happy person will never make you feel unhappy about yourself.

You gave your all to that person.
And they kept taking.
But we all have only so much to give.

Student: Does this mean that I should not be guilty of walking out of a toxic relationship, even though the relationship also had layers of love?

Teacher: You know the answer to this question.

Student: But how do I manage guilt and loneliness together?

Teacher: That is where journaling is immensely powerful, where you keep a note of all your emotions.

When you felt his toxicity at the deepest level.
When you felt loved by the things he did.
When you felt alone even in his presence.
When he comforted you by simply texting.

This journal will help you reflect on the daily emotions and experiences you went through.
Both good and bad.
Especially the bad, because you need to be reminded of them when you have broken up.

Student: So this recording of my emotions is a reminder to myself, to bring me back to reality?

Teacher: Exactly.
Because right now your mind just craves his presence. It has forgotten what it felt like to be with him.

Student: Once the emotions fade away, are you suggesting I will not miss him?

Teacher: There is no harm in missing him as long as it doesn't stop you from loving yourself. It is possible that you love him as a person, but you never loved the relationship you were in. And that is why you chose to step away from it.

Student: So if the emotions are temporary, I should not take any permanent decisions based on them.

Teacher (smiling): The teacher has appeared!

How Do I Set Boundaries?

Student: I find it really hard to set boundaries. We all want them. Yet we hardly get people to respect them.
Why does that happen?

Teacher: There are deeper reasons for it, which we will uncover.
However, before that, an important thing to know is why are boundaries important in the first place.

They are important because everyone has their own definition of how the world works. Let's say a friend of yours loves laughing out loud. If you are also someone who loves laughing out loud, that's great.
If, on the other hand, you are someone who does not appreciate that, it will sound rude to you.

Neither is right or wrong.

They are just preferences.

And some preferences are non-negotiable.

I would call them boundaries.

Student: Could we also call them differences of opinion?

Teacher: They *are* differences of opinion.

And the most beautiful thing about these differences is they can coexist without intruding on the other person's opinion.

Student: How is that possible?

When we set and respect our boundaries, we also encourage others to create and respect theirs.

Teacher: Think of the way houses have physical boundaries.

Each house has a space within which its members build their habitat.

By doing so, it also allows another house to have its own physical space without intruding on anyone else's.

But both do meet, they do engage and they do interact.

While still setting their own boundaries.

Student: So boundaries allow space for everyone else as well?

Teacher: Right.

Which is why boundaries are so important in relationships as well.

People who love each other are still different people with different perspectives and different priorities.

Student: How do we start setting boundaries?

Teacher: It starts with understanding that it is going to be a difficult conversation.

Because when you are setting boundaries with people you love – could be friends, partners, parents – you are essentially saying that here is where my space starts and your space ends.

As a culture, that is not something we are used to listening to.

It is something we do not feel right about!

And we all have seen the repercussions of that, taking us for granted because we expected them to hear the unspoken.

They were not wrong in intruding into the boundary because in their head it didn't even exist!

Student: Yes, it makes me think of some instances where my boundary was intruded and I kept expecting them to respect it.

Teacher: We know ourselves through our thoughts.

Others know us through our actions.

If our actions (in this case, conversations) do not speak up for what we want, all we are saying is that we do not want anything.

Student: But if they love me so much, can they not understand what I want?

Teacher: Because they love you so much, all they understand is that you will open up about what you want.

Student: But I am not rigid regarding my boundaries.

Some things are an absolute must for me, but with some others, I am flexible.

Is it also possible to have spaces where I am not willing to compromise and spaces where some bit of adjustment is okay?

Teacher: Absolutely.

It is how non-negotiable and negotiable boundaries operate.

They are a healthy balance of self-love and infinite love for the other person.

Student: Can you give me some examples of how they can coexist?

Teacher: Let's say you do not want to have any conversations around politics or religion. That is a non-negotiable boundary.

Or you do not ever want to be around someone who is disrespectful to others.

That is another non-negotiable boundary. You will not compromise these boundaries in any relationship.

Until you learn to respect your boundaries,
nobody else will.

A negotiable boundary could be punctuality, where you like to show up on time, but if the other person does not show up on time, that would not be the reason to break that relationship.

Student: It requires such a tremendous level of self-awareness!

Teacher: That is where most of us falter.

Most of us aren't aware of what we want, yet we expect everyone else to respect what we want.

When we are not aware of what we want, we, sadly, become narcissists in our most important relationships.

Student: Oh, I can understand how relationships become so complicated despite everyone's best intentions.

Teacher: Reminds me of the lead character in the sitcom *Big Bang Theory*, where he gets into a 'Roommate Agreement' – the dos and don'ts of being his roommate.

As stupid and funny as it was shown to be, the truth is that these agreements work like a charm.

Student: They would work for the relationships we choose.

For our family, which are the relationships we didn't choose, it almost looks like the concept of boundaries is a joke.

Teacher: I agree it might look futile to create boundaries with family.
However, what is the harm in trying?

If it does not work out and you see the lack of boundaries harming you, get financially independent and consider moving out. Sometimes moving out physically is the best way to save your relationship with your parents.

Student: So boundaries are not selfish demands.
If communicated well, they can be the reason for us to never feel the need to be selfish. Right?

Teacher (smiling): The teacher has appeared!

How Do I Deal with Toxic Friends?

Student: I have a feeling that one of my friends has turned toxic.
But I don't know for sure.
Is there a way to find out?

Teacher: The reality, my friend, is no one becomes toxic on purpose.
As much as people do not want to, some still end up becoming unhealthy for us.

Student: Why does that happen?

Teacher: We all are attracted to people who do not have what we have.
Not just in terms of physical possessions but personality traits as well.
The early excitement of meeting someone new, getting to know them, forming a friendship – all makes it really hard for us to know the true person inside.

The true person emerges in time.
What started as a beautiful bond could transform into something undesirable.

Student: That makes me sad.

Teacher: Which is why we must understand that toxicity is an emotion.
Not a source of truth.
Two people who are toxic for each other could very well be wonderful as individuals.

It is not always the person.
It is the emotion that the relationship generates that makes the bond toxic.

Student: So how should I deal with it?

Teacher: Any friendship that harms you – emotionally, mentally, psychologically – is a feeling you live through.
That feeling should prompt you to look into yourself and explore it.
What is it that is disturbing me?

What do I want to protect?

Why is it such an important value to me?

What part of me is it pointing towards?

The toxicity you feel in a relationship is an opportunity to understand your relationship with yourself.

This conversation will lead you to an eventual question: What are these emotions trying to tell me about myself?

Student: Why would someone else's toxicity tell me something about myself?

Teacher: Difficult situations do not test us.
They reveal us.

Think of happiness.
Let's say your value system is to be responsible for your happiness. If someone else holds you responsible for their happiness, the friendship becomes toxic.
Until you do not know this fact about yourself, you will never realize what it is about the other person's behaviour that makes the relationship toxic.

Student: So in a way people become toxic when their needs are not met. Is that correct?

Teacher: Isn't that the truth?
No one wakes up one fine morning with the agenda 'I will screw up another human being's life', yet they do. Because, they crave their needs to be met by others.

Student: Is there a way to heal this unmet need?

Teacher: Once you know what makes the friendship toxic, you heal it through conversation.

You sit and talk with them and honestly admit what you feel.

Student: What would the conversation look like?

Teacher: An honest conversation with your friend on how this friendship is affecting you.

You do not complain.

You do not accuse.

You do not offer solutions.

You simply share what you feel.

And allow them to hear you out.

The conversation will reveal a lot.

About both of you.

You will realize where you have to change; your friend will realize where they have to change.

Student: What if they do not want to change?

Teacher: Maybe the other person does not want to change. Maybe you do not want to change.

Perhaps the conclusion is that what worked in the past may not work now.

And you decide to move on instead of holding on to something that is draining you both.

Maybe the other person does want to change.
Maybe you actually want to change.
Then both of you start working towards reimagining the relationship.

It may not be easy, but it is what will liberate you eventually.

Student: I have a follow-up question.
Whenever we start any new friendship, it does not begin as toxic.
It is only in time that we realize it has become that way.
Is there a way to know whether a friendship may become toxic in the future or not?

Teacher: The truth in almost every friendship is that you are not able to see clearly what this friendship can lead you into.

However, whenever you figure out the not-so-good side of that friendship, the question is: What do you do about it?

Student: As you mentioned, we talk about it. And maybe move away if it doesn't work out.

Teacher: We would all be wandering lonely if we walked away from all our friendships at the slightest difficulty.

We can learn from this experience.

We reflect on the traits of the other person that were always visible, but we chose to ignore.

And it then becomes our responsibility to be aware of this in all future relationships.

We learn from our mistakes.

Student: That's a lot of work.

Teacher: Who else would do it for you?

Student: Tell me something. So far, our conversation suggests that the fault or change may lie in the other person. What if that isn't the case? And the fault lies in me? How do I know that I am the toxic one?

Teacher: The conversation with your friend will make you aware.

DEALING WITH TOXIC FRIENDS

Having problems in friendship

↓

Know what needs to be fixed

↓

Solve it by sharing your emotions and having an honest conversation

Things get better, you both feel better and the problem gets fixed

You both discover a lot of things about yourselves and gather the courage to end it

Student: And once I become aware of it?

Teacher: Then remind yourself of why you entered into this friendship in the first place.
Because it made you happy.
Because you wanted to be happy in it.
So do everything that you need to do to be happy in it again.
This simple yardstick solves everything – how can I make the relationship happy again?

Student: That will be my biggest takeaway.
How can I make the friendship happy again?
It may mean walking out.
It may mean working on myself.
Whatever it takes.
No?

Teacher (smiling): The teacher has appeared!

PART 4

MANAGING YOURSELF

How Do I Develop Patience?

Student: I lack patience. I need everything right now.

Teacher: Do you know of anyone who is patient?

Student: I find my parents zen-like.
My father will not check his WhatsApp for hours. And my mom is perfectly fine waiting for the product to come 1–2 days later, unlike me who would want it in the next 15 minutes. I find them living a very peaceful life.

How are they so patient?

Teacher: When your parents were kids, they had no option but to be patient.
Letters used to take days and weeks to get delivered.

You had to stand in line to get basics such as milk or vegetables.

You had to book an interstate or international call in advance.

Even buying cars, scooters, watches was always on the waitlist, extending to months and years.

So they knew what it was to wait.

Student: So patience was something they were trained to have?

But why is it my fault if I live at a time when everything is available at the click of a button?

Teacher: I get you, I totally get you. It isn't your fault.

However, what isn't your fault is still your responsibility.

You were not trained to be patient.

But that doesn't mean you should not be patient.

What isn't your fault is still your responsibility. Just because you didn't create the problem doesn't mean you don't solve the problem.

Student: Oh wow. So I have to become patient by force?

Teacher: When you say it like that, it sounds like a chore.
You have to get comfortable with waiting for things to happen.

Student: How?

Teacher: Start with basic things.
If you really want something badly today, wait for 30 days.

And then ask yourself after 30 days if you still need that thing.
There are high chances you won't.

If you feel hungry, resist ordering right away. Wait for another 60 minutes and ask yourself if you are still hungry.
There are high chances you were looking at food simply as entertainment.

Student: Will just waiting for something make me patient?

Teacher: By waiting for something physical to arrive, you unconsciously fight the mental conflict to fulfil your desires instantly.
As you build this muscle, you begin to get patient with people as well.
Or when things do not happen when you want them to happen.

Student: The plan sounds practical, but is there no other way?

If the world around us is designed in a manner that rewards everything instantly, why do I have to go against the flow?

Teacher: You are not going against the flow. You are going with the right flow of understanding life, which says that most good things in life take time.

It takes time to find good friends.
It takes time to build meaningful relationships.
It takes time to be successful at a job.
Think of life like compound interest. It magnifies everything you put in with consistency.

Student: But how does it actually work?
It always feels like nothing is moving, so my brain craves instant rewards.

Teacher: That is how we are designed.

We crave the easy because that fulfils us instantly.

But once we have achieved that, we realize we are still discontented.

So we crave for more.

And the cycle continues.

You have to essentially fight the basic instinct of your mind, which is to seek pleasure.

It seeks pleasure through likes, comments and shares on social media, through 30-minute delivery of your food order, binge-watching an entire series and one-night stands.

It is proven through research that the ones who can resist the urge of the instant, the ones who can delay the gratification for a bigger gratification later, go on to win big in life.

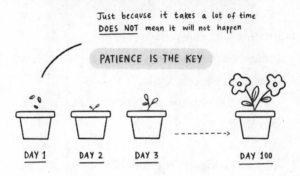

WHAT DEVELOPING PATIENCE LOOKS LIKE

Just because it takes a lot of time **DOES NOT** mean it will not happen

PATIENCE IS THE KEY

DAY 1   DAY 2   DAY 3   → DAY 100

Student: So then, why do so many successful people glorify the hustle culture?

Always be working.

Always be fighting.

Always be thinking.

We are asked to be on a perpetual on mode

How does patience fit in here?

Teacher: Impatient with your actions. Patient with results.

If you know what needs to be done, then do it right away. Be impatient with that.

But do not be impatient with what it yields.
Because that seed might take time to flower.

Student: Oh, now I connect.
It may take years of relentless hard work before any results show.
Reserve the impatience for the hard work, not the result.

Teacher (smiling): The teacher has appeared!

How Can I Have a Sleep Routine?

Student: Why is sleep given so much importance? I am young, I want to live life to the max, sometimes not even sleep!

Teacher: Go back to when you were a kid.
As a toddler, you had a fixed bedtime, eating time, playtime, etc.
As a kid growing up, you had the same – school time, self-study at home, playtime, bedtime, etc.

What do you think those routines did to you as a kid?

Student: I hated those routines!

Teacher (smiles): I understand. But what did they end up doing for you, though?

Student: Well, they ensured I got to do everything – whether it is fun, sports, sleep or studies.

Teacher: That is the power of routine.
You might hate it when it is in place.
But you love it for the results it brings.
Which is exactly what happens with a healthy sleep routine.

No one loves adhering to routines. But everyone LOVES the results routines bring.

The world is young. The world is shiny. The 'cool' world 'doesn't sleep'.
Except that biologically we need sleep.
Sleep that serves our mind and body the right way.

Student: But shouldn't we make room for spontaneity?

Teacher: I'd agree.
Be mindful though not to confuse randomness with spontaneity.
Spontaneity leads to creativity, for which we must make room.
However, not having a schedule, particularly a sleep schedule, is deceiving ourselves under the mask of productivity.

Student: How is that different, and can we even 'schedule' spontaneity?

Teacher: Think of it like going to a park every evening once you are done with your work.
You just go there without your phone, and you let yourself unwind. That is your routine.
You are 100% certain to not come up with the same thoughts every day.
They will be random.
That is the spontaneity we scheduled for.
By having a routine.

But when you do not have a routine, going to the park will be replaced with tasks not done and worries not solved.

Student: Will having a healthy sleep routine fix that?

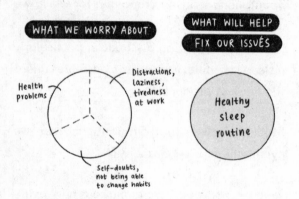

Teacher: Having a healthy sleep routine is the foundation of what you want to do for the rest of the day.
A healthy sleep routine starts with sleeping on time.

Every single day of the week.

You plan your day.
You fix your bedtime.
And you stay true to it.
Like clockwork.

Student: And why is it important to sleep at the same time every day?

Teacher: To tell our body that it is time.
To respect its need to rest.

Student: That makes a lot of sense. Tell me something, what if some days I am delayed due to work?

Teacher: Such days, by design, should be few. Else they are consuming your day already!

Student: That is so true! What else do I need to know?

Teacher: What do you do in the last 30–60 minutes before you go to bed?

Student: My usual way of sleeping is to unwind by watching an hour of reels on YouTube or Netflix. Helps me unwind.

Teacher: That will make sure your sleep cycle is anything but fixed.

Student: Sorry?

Teacher: You should be. To yourself.
When you watch something that stimulates your senses, your body gets no signal that it is time to unwind. Instead, you are feeding it with emotions that spark even further emotions. Laughter leads to surprise leads to fear leads to sadness leads to sorrow.

The right approach is to not have contact with the screen at least 60 minutes prior to sleeping. Calm your body down. Not activate it.

Student: But what do I do if I do not use my phone before sleeping?

Teacher: Anything that doesn't activate your senses.

Reading books is a beautiful way. But the right books. Not thrillers. Not fantasy. Not hard-hitting philosophy.

Perhaps poetry. Perhaps a simple story.

Or journaling.

Or soft music that soothes you.

Student: So sleeping at the same time every day is one. What else?

Teacher: Waking up slowly.

We often wake up just in time for our day. Just in time for our classes, just in time for our bus, just in time for our meeting/call.

Doing so leads to an imbalanced mind and body.

We remain in a state of self-inflicted urgency.

Wake up slowly.

It could be by drinking a glass of water or chanting your affirmations or just breathing in the morning air.

Student: Oh, so for a night of sleep to be good, the day needs to start in a good way as well.

Teacher: The start of the day is critical to how the rest of the day goes.

Student: I know what you are saying is right. But when I see my friends with no sleep routine having fun every night, I give in to the temptation.

Teacher: If it happens rarely, I do not think that is a bad thing to do.
However, if it is something that happens often, you know the answer.

Student: Could it also be that such friends are harmful?
Do they make me feel bad for being myself?

Teacher: You are wise enough to know the answer by now.

Student: One more thing I struggle with is waking up on time. I wake up at 8 a.m. everyday, but I wish to wake up at 6 a.m. What should I do?

Teacher: What have you done so far?

Student: Set an alarm for 6 a.m.

Teacher: And let me guess. It worked wonderfully for a few days. And then it stopped working. You went back to 8 a.m.

Student: Was it so obvious?

Teacher: It's obvious because everyone makes the same mistake. Shock our body into change.
Our body adapts well to slow change.
So if you wish to get up at 6 a.m. instead of 8 a.m., start slow.

Student: How?

Teacher: Set your alarm for 7.50 a.m.

Your body will not even notice the 10-minute difference. But it is a material first step.

Do it for 3 weeks, and your body will get used to it.

Once used to it, set the alarm for 7.40 a.m.

Again 3 weeks.

Then 7.30 a.m.

Again 3 weeks.

In a few weeks you will get to 6 a.m.

Most importantly, your body would not have fought the change, instead it would have adapted to the change slowly.

Student: Does this really work?

Teacher: It worked for me. From 7 a.m. I now wake up at 4.30 a.m.

Student: And let me guess. It took you several years to get there? But you were okay with it, because it is a small price to pay for a lifetime of good habits?

Teacher (smiling): The teacher has appeared!

How Do I Build Good Habits?

Student: I have tried so much to form good habits – hit the gym, eat the right food in the right proportions, call my parents. Yet, I have failed so badly.

Is there a secret sauce to building good habits?

Teacher: Yes, there is a secret sauce to forming the right habits.

But before that, it is very important to understand why habits work.

Our brain is designed in a manner that it wants to consume the least amount of energy to accomplish tasks and activities.

Its goal is to conserve energy.

To dispense it minimally.

Habits are things you do repeatedly so your brain can do them on autopilot.

Student: So we have to get ourselves to a place where whatever task we wish to accomplish becomes a habit. So that it is easier for the brain to do the task than not to do it.

Teacher: True.
One way to build a habit easily is to make it gradual. Small steps at a time.
Let's say you wish to form the habit of getting up at 5 a.m. instead of the usual 8 a.m. How would you build that?

Student: Set an alarm for 5 a.m. every day!

Teacher: How often does it help?

Student: Helps for two days.
Day 3, and I am back to 8.15 a.m.

Teacher: Because you put your body in a position to resist that change.
For that habit to be effective, your body must adapt to it.

Student: But the body will never approve of such a huge change in my waking-up time.

Teacher: That is why you trick your brain and your body to make small changes so that it consumes the least amount of energy.

Habits that give big results start small. Because they are a consequence of pleasure, not pressure.

Student: How do you do that?

Teacher: If you wake up at 8 a.m. right now, set your alarm for 7.50 a.m. for the next day. The body won't even come to know of such a small change. Hence, the brain will also consume very little energy to make that little change possible.

Do so for the next three weeks.

Once your body has adapted to it, bring that waking time to 7.40 a.m. for the next three weeks.

Over a period of time, you will adapt yourself to the new habit and graduate towards the eventual one, with little resistance from the body.

Student: By this logic, it will take almost a year to get to 5 a.m.!

Teacher: You have tried instant ways and failed for years.

Why not try gradual ways and have a permanent habit in a year?

Student: That makes sense.

Especially because it does not require me to make big changes.

Teacher: Consistency matters more than intensity.

Student: But what is wrong if I start the big thing today itself?

Teacher: You will not have the energy to get back to it the next day. Your mind and body will crave the original. It will find solace in it. Because, remember, the brain would give you all possible excuses to conserve its energy.

Student: Let's say I have accomplished this.
Is this enough? How do I find the motivation to keep progressing, even if they are small steps?
The mind will eventually know, right?

Teacher: IF the mind is smart, it will.
Which is where you bring in the element that motivates the mind.
A sense of progress!

Think about it this way – why are you even going through this trouble of building a good habit?

It must be for a gain, right?

For example, why do you want to wake up early? You must have some motive.

Student: Yes, there is. I have always wanted to play a sport but never found the time. I know of a swimming club near my place which I would love to join. But the class happens at 6 a.m. So I have to wake up earlier to attend the class.

Teacher: Great. You have a motive. We all do. Without a motive, there will never be a habit. Your goal is to measure your progress towards that motive.

And feed your brain with that progress.

If our brain feels progress, it yearns to do more of what makes it progress.

Quicker than you know, you have reached a better place than you had expected.

Student: But habits cannot replace goals.

Teacher: I would argue that they should.

Student: But aren't goals necessary to motivate us?

Teacher: I think goals are restricting.
If you hit them, you feel great about them.
But what if you could have gone beyond but you stopped?
If you do not hit them, you feel terrible about yourself. But what if you were never in the best position to hit them in the first place?
Both these extreme emotions are unwarranted.
I think we often translate our desires into goals.
I am, instead, a fan of habits.
Keep doing the right things consistently.

Keep getting a little better each time.
Show up even when you don't feel like it (because you are habituated to it).
And you will reach goals you could not have imagined for yourself.

Student: This is so cool!
I have experienced that in places where I do not set goals, whether it is my reading habit or journaling every night, I get better at those habits because I do not have a destination.
I have completed more books in a year than I could have imagined and written more words than a usual book would have!

Teacher: I am not surprised.

Student: What if we live in an environment where the temptation to go back to your original mode is very high? How do I build the motivation to resist?

Teacher: The most motivated person eliminates all negative stimuli that stop them from taking action.

Let's say you want to get fit.
But you wake up in the morning and tell yourself, 'No, I have to go downstairs and go to the gym. I'll be embarrassing myself in front of everyone else. But I have to travel next week. Will start after coming back. Also, I didn't sleep well last night. I'd better go to sleep now.' Classic excuses.

What if you order weights at home?
What if you sign up for an online class?
What if you eliminate the excuses?
Instead of trying to motivate yourself to build the right habit, make it easy to build the right habit.

Get rid of cigarettes in your home if you want to stop smoking.
Get rid of cold drinks if you want to eliminate sugar.

Get rid of the food ordering apps if you do not want to binge-eat.

Eliminate all distractions that come in the way of you and your new habit.

THE POWER OF MAKING SMALL CHANGES
WHILE BUILDING NEW HABITS

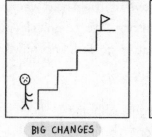

BIG CHANGES

SMALL CHANGES

Student: That makes a lot of sense.

I have a newfound appreciation for habits as a way of achieving way more than what I could have set out for myself.

And it starts by eliminating distractions. Because I can!

Teacher (smiling): The teacher has appeared!

How Can I Be More Self-aware?

Student: How do you have such clarity of thought? I would like to become you.

Teacher: Thank you! Self-awareness is being intensely aware of why you do things in the first place.
The more awareness you have of the 'why', the more you will know what works for you and what doesn't.

Unless you know why you do something in the first place, you won't be able to change it.

Student: It sounds great to hear.
But how does this apply practically in life?

Teacher: Think about failures.

Everyone in the world fails.

But not everyone succeeds.

Why is it then that we call failures stepping stones to success?

Because the ones who succeeded eventually after failing reflected on their failures. Instead of quickly moving on, they asked themselves multiple questions:

- What I thought was true, but now I know is not?
- What I thought was false, but now I know is not?
- What is this trying to teach me?
- What will I change from tomorrow, basis the responses above?

Student: But I still wonder how this works?

Teacher: It works because reflection makes us pause.

But we all hate to reflect, to pause.

We are scared of what we might discover when we sit to reflect.

This is true for life.
Whenever you feel stuck, feel helpless, feel directionless, sit with yourself.
Meditate on what you need to do in life in order to move ahead.
You WILL find an answer.
The answer will not be the one you like, but it will certainly be the one you need.

Student: So most people get comfortable avoiding rather than being aware. Is that the right way to put it?

Teacher: Yes. It's the sad truth.
The answer will require effort.
It will require commitment.
It will also require you to shift your way of living and behaviour.
That is why it is going to be uncomfortable.

Student: But is that the only way to become self-aware?

Teacher: What do you think?

Student: I don't know.

Teacher: There are a lot of students who reach out to me saying,
'I am confused. What should I do?'

Student: And you give them the same uncomfortable answer. Isn't it?

Teacher: The last thing a good teacher does is serve answers on a platter.
I ask them, 'What's stopping you from doing what you know you should do?'

Student: If everyone knows what they should do, why don't they do it?

Teacher: Fear.
Fear of failure.

Fear of being compared to others.
Fear of rejection.
Fear of reprimand.
Fear of the unknown.
Even fear of success.

That fear stops them from asking themselves: What is really stopping me from facing that fear?

Student: And if they eventually ask themselves, do they face their fear?

Teacher: The moment they ask themselves this question, they take the first step towards awareness.
Then it becomes a journey.
Just like the journey of fitness.
You have to undertake it daily to call yourself fit.
It is a journey, not a destination.
No one can ever say 'I am fit'; they can only claim 'I remain fit'.
The day you end the journey, you eventually stop being fit.

Student: So, many people are caught in a rut, and still complain about their life not changing. How is it possible that they know how to get out and yet they continue to live in that rut?

Teacher: Here is the shocking truth.
The rut is their comfort.
Because it allows them to complain.
It allows them to believe everything is someone else's fault.
It allows them to believe that the world owes them something.
The ones not in a relationship think those who are in relationships owe them something. The ones working in a company think the company owes them something.

Their belief system is driven by the fact that had someone else behaved the right way or had something else worked out for them, their world would have been a better one.

Student: How does one even realize this and become self-aware?

Teacher: When someone is ready to take the journey of self-awareness, they will recognize the need for it.
It will emerge by itself.
You cannot push someone to be self-aware.

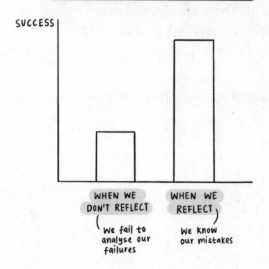

SUCCESS AND PERSONAL REFLECTION

SUCCESS

WHEN WE DON'T REFLECT
(we fail to analyse our failures

WHEN WE REFLECT)
We know our mistakes

Student: It is just like helping.
You cannot help someone who does not want to be helped.

Teacher: Even if you know you can. Even if they know you can.

Student: I think this journey of self-awareness is best undertaken as early as possible.
Over time, it will become a habit.
And the next thing you know – facing the truth is the default mode for you.
No?

Teacher (smiling): The teacher has appeared!

How Can I Live by Myself?

Student: To live by yourself is both magical yet miserable, don't you think? Magical because you experience freedom for the first time. Miserable because sometimes you end up misusing that freedom or mismanaging it. I wonder if there is a middle way.

Teacher: When you start living by yourself, you experience three aspects of your life – money, health and relationships.

Let's start with money.
When you were at your home, you never thought about something as fundamental as which toothpaste to use, what utensils/appliances to have, what to cook, how the house gets cleaned every day – all of it happened without you being even aware of anything.

But when you move out of your home for college or your job, you will have no choice but to make all these decisions from Day 1.

Student: I don't even know where to start.

Teacher: By creating a budget.
A budget for your money – base it on what you need to do, what you want to do and what you have to do.

What you need to do are your needs. Your essentials.
This includes your rent, your food, your bills, your help.
Everything that you need to spend to just survive.

What you want to do are your desires.
This includes your clothes, your parties, your vacations, your phones.
Everything that you wish to spend on to enjoy your life.

What you have to do are your investments.
This includes health insurance, life insurance,
emergency funds and investing for the future.

Student: This is so helpful.
How much should I spend on each category?

Teacher: A good guiding principle is called the
50:30:20 rule.
50% of your monthly income should be
towards your needs (and no more)
Be as thrifty as you can in this.
30% of your monthly income should be
towards your wants (and no more)
20% at least of your monthly income should
be towards your investments.

So the moment you get your salary credited,
you shift a minimum of 20% of it into a
separate bank account and invest it and use
the remaining 80% for your needs and wants.

Student: But that iPhone I want will never come in that 30%. It costs 90% of my current salary.

Teacher: In that case, you continue saving that sum over the months so that it fulfils what you want.
You cannot afford an iPhone today. But you can in 3 months if you saved all of your 30% allocation.
Or in 6 months, if you saved half of it while still spending half on other desires.

Student: That requires a lot of discipline.

Teacher: Everything good does!

Planning is easy. Execution requires discipline.

Student: Are you already hinting towards the second aspect of living by yourself?

Teacher: Yes! Health.
The biggest thing that goes for a toss when we live by ourselves is health.
When we are at home, we used to think that our parents are restrictive and acting miserly by not allowing us to order food.
All we had every day were boring homemade meals.
But they were simply making sure that you ate healthy while not spending unnecessarily.

Student: I do order food a couple of times a week since I live away from my parents.
The things that you say about becoming unhealthy – I don't see it.
I still look the same as I used to.

Teacher: The truth about bad health habits is that you do not see any effects of the abuse in your 20s.

It is when you enter your 30s that you start to experience the consequences of your decisions.

Some of those consequences may set you back by decades.

Student: Hmm.
So does this mean I should not enjoy my food?

Teacher: You absolutely must.
But if you are eating only for enjoyment, then it is anything but enjoyment.

Student: I need to reflect upon this further.

Teacher: While you do, let me move on to the third aspect that becomes our responsibility when we start living by ourselves – relationships.

Most of your relationships while staying with parents were relationships by birth (your relatives) or those that were supervised by your parents (your friends).

You never truly experienced independence in your relationships.

But now you will.

And this independence can get to our head. We may tend to get into relationships that harm us.

Student: How do I know that?

Teacher: You will start spending time with people because of how they make you look in front of others instead of who they truly are. You begin to talk about people and not ideas.

Student: How do I avoid these relationship mistakes?

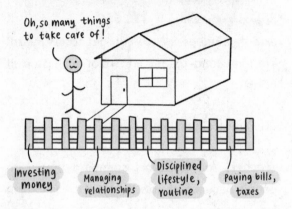

Teacher: You start with not rebounding immediately after a relationship failure.

Rather, you stop, pause and reflect upon why you got into that relationship in the first place.

What unfulfilled need of yours did that relationship fulfil?

This level of awareness comes only when you spend time with yourself, which will eventually make you better at making choices in relationships.

People aren't 'good' or 'bad' per se; someone who is an angel to one may be a nightmare to another.

Our temperament defines how our relationships make us feel.

Student: All of this seems so overwhelming. Why is it so important to take care of yourself so much when you live by yourself?

Teacher: Because you will be by yourself now for the rest of your life.

Even when you form other relationships, you will only truly have yourself to call upon.

Everyone else is merely an observer.

But they can never know what you are going through.

Until you do not learn how to live by yourself, with yourself, you will continue to look for others in your life to complete your life.

Student: I think our conversations have time and time again reminded me of this.

I am the only one for myself.

I find that living by yourself brings with it a lot of FOMO.

What if I do not go out and post that food picture on my Instagram?

I do not have the money to go on a trip with my friends but what do I tell them?

Will I be the party spoiler if I choose to take care of my health and not eat what we order at the restaurant?

Will it affect my relationships as well?

These questions keep bothering me.

Teacher: Living by yourself will eventually teach you how to deal with these questions.

Let's say your friends want you to eat out.

You eat something before you go and that fills you up.

So when you get to the restaurant, you eat in a limited manner.

Surprise, surprise: Over time, everyone will come to accept that you eat only this much.

If you are invited for a vacation, you want to go but also want to take care of your monthly budget; you go for 2–3 days instead of the entire vacation.
Go towards the end so that no one can force you to stay longer.

There are no straightforward answers. We all make them up along the way. As you will too.

Student: Becoming an adult is quite scary.
I miss the innocence of my childhood days, the comfort of home, even my parents scolding me. But I know that life moves on.
In some way, dealing with adulthood will be my way of loving myself, knowing that I tried to do a good job of it.
No?

Teacher (smiling): The teacher has appeared!

How Do I Manage My Anger?

Student: Sometimes, the smallest of things make me angry. When I reflect upon them later, I feel angrier. Is there a way to manage my anger?

Teacher: All our emotions have a reason.

Anger, for instance, surfaces when a very important need of ours is not met.

On the surface of it, someone lied, and it made you angry.

However, when you scratch the surface, you may find that you felt stupid to have believed the lie.

And stupid is something you do not ever want to feel!

THAT feeling made you angry.

Not the lie.

But the sense of feeling stupid.

Student: But don't people get angry when someone hits their car?

What about two random people fighting for a seat in public transport?

Or two colleagues getting angry with their strict manager?

Do these petty things also have unresolved issues?

I don't think so . . .

Teacher: The car owner is angry with the one who hit his car because he was scolded as a kid for breaking even a tiny cup.

That tiny scratch took him to his childhood where he was told 'it's NOT okay' if things broke while he played.

Two random people fight for a seat in public transport because they have been working intensely hard and believe they deserve something in life.
But it is not coming.

Not easily.

Colleagues get angry with a manager who is strict and wants them to become more disciplined because to them strictness as a kid meant having zero freedom, obeying rules and stifling their curiosity.

Anger's purpose is to make us aware of an unresolved need.
The moment we become aware of that need, anger has served its purpose.

Student: Oh, so unresolved issues crop up as anger?

Teacher: All the time.
You feel triggered and angry by something personal to you.

Student: How do you eliminate it?

Teacher: 3 steps.
Step 1 – Recognize that you are about to get angry.
Anger is a strong emotion.
We all know how it feels.
We can all sense it even before it comes.

Step 2 – Count to ten and take deep breaths.
It sounds funny, but it works.
Calm down.
DO NOT react at that moment.
You have, at that moment, won half the battle by recognizing you are about to get angry.
You are already an observer.
Now let that anger go past you.
Recall our conversation about meditation when you sit by the roadside watching cars go by?

Anger is one such car.

You see it, you see what's inside, you notice its colour, its speed, its make.

But you don't stop it or get into it.

You simply watch it go past you.

Student: You do realize I am not you?

Teacher: You do not have to become anybody to do this.

It will come by itself.

It will come with practice.

There will be enough moments during the day when you feel anger emerge.

Don't get angry.

Begin to observe it.

Start with small incidents, where it will be relatively easier to let go of the anger.

Student: Let's say I do. This way I will keep getting angry and never express myself. How does it fix the core issue that I get angry often?

Teacher: Which brings me to Step 3.

Understand your anger.

All anger stems from an unfulfilled need.

Uncover that need.

Student: How?

Teacher: That is personal.

For some, it could be through writing a journal.

For some, through a conversation with themselves.

For some, through therapy.

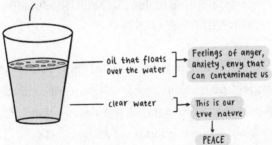

A REPRESENTATION OF OUR FEELINGS

IMAGINE YOURSELF AS THIS GLASS OF WATER

oil that floats over the water ⟶ Feelings of anger, anxiety, envy that can contaminate us

clear water ⟶ This is our true nature ⟶ PEACE

Student: Remind me again, why do I need to go through this? How does identifying this unfulfilled need help my anger?

Teacher: Go back to where we started.
Every emotion is there to serve a purpose.
Anger's purpose is to warn you.
And get you to defend yourself.
You realize that your unfulfilled need is surfacing.
And anger is activated to prepare you for it.
To make you realize that this need is unfulfilled.
And that a certain person or situation is provoking it.
Do something about it.
Anger is shouting at you, 'DO YOU REMEMBER THAT NEED OF YOURS?'

The second you realize what that need is, anger goes, 'Oh cool – you remember? Awesome. I am done. I will now go back to chilling. Have a good day, you lovely.'

And anger will be gone!

Student: Come on! This is not how it works.

Teacher: I understand that this is hard to believe.
But there is only one way to find out.

Student: This reminds me of the scene from the movie *Matrix*.
'No one can be told what the Matrix is. You have to see it for yourself.'
That is how it is, isn't it? These 3 steps to manage anger.

Teacher (smiling): The teacher has appeared!

How Can I Pick Myself Up?

Student: As a kid, it was so easy to pick yourself up after a fall. As an adult, I struggle to do it.

Teacher: Should you not be accustomed to it by now?

Student: Absolutely.
But it is weird, isn't it? It seems I have forgotten what I knew as a kid.

Teacher: What made you forget the art of picking yourself up?

Student: Perhaps the belief that life gets difficult with time and you actually cannot pick yourself up.

Teacher: That is exactly the reason you do not feel like a kid any more.
The biggest reason you feel like a failure is

that you are not sure whether you will ever
get a shot again at winning.

You feel like a failure because you are not sure of winning again.

Student: That's sad but true.
How to get over this?

Teacher: You do not need to get over it.
You simply need to remind yourself that failing
simply means a failure in the journey.
Not in the eventual outcome.

Student: I understand that there is more to
life than just this failure.
But it still feels like a struggle to pick myself
up.

Teacher: We feel like a failure because we think we cannot get to a point of winning again.

But the strange thing about winning is that it isn't about winning. It is about a feeling of progress.

Student: Explain this a bit more.

Teacher: Sure.
Say you are playing a game of badminton with an opponent, and you are down by a score of 1–7.
A friend passes by and asks for your score.
You are embarrassed at that moment.
You feel like a failure.
Sheepishly you share the score.
Your friend doesn't read too much into it and moves on after saying some comforting words, 'Don't worry, keep playing'.

You eventually lose the match, but you lose it 8–10.

The same friend passes by and, out of courtesy, asks you the score again.

This time, though, is different.

You are now filled with a sense of pride.

You say you lost 8–10.

What just happened here?

You lost, and yet you felt good about yourself?

You lost, and yet you moved from feeling like a failure to feeling like you won something?

How?

Student: This is so fascinating. So true.

I would actually feel like a winner at that moment, even though I lost.

Teacher: Because you experienced progress.

Because you realized you can win if you keep at it.

Student: Does this mean we don't have to win every time to feel good about ourselves?

Teacher: Absolutely.

Winning is not the purpose of life.

To get better at living it, is.

And this sense of progress is what will pick you up whenever you are down.

Student: So most of our inability to pick ourselves up comes from this lack of progress?

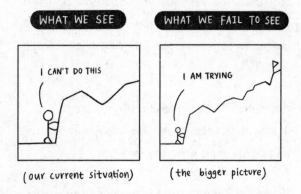

(our current sitvation)   (the bigger picture)

Teacher: The only progress we know of is the end result.

Clearing the exam.

Winning the award.

Getting to that bank balance.
We tend to see the destination as progress.
But it is the journey that shows your progress.

Getting better at retaining facts is the progress you make towards passing the exam.
Getting your work done on time and improving upon the feedback you receive is the progress you make towards winning the award.
Investing every month and watching your money compound is the progress towards getting to that bank balance.

Student: Incredible!
As you say this, I realize that every time I faced a setback, I almost always relied on something external to pick me up.
Maybe my parents, my friends, at times even luck.
I just hoped something would get me out of this rut.
But this conversation tells me that the power to pick myself lies within me.

And if I feel I am progressing, I will still feel like a winner, even though I may not yet have won!
No?

Teacher (smiling): The teacher has appeared!

How Can I Become My Best Friend?

Student: Nowadays it is quite cool to quote this concept of self-love.

'Become your own best friend' is what people say.

But is it possible to become your own best friend?

Teacher: Define 'best friend'.

Student: Someone who is there for us, no matter what.

Someone who knows us very well.

They know our strengths and help us build on them.

They also know our weaknesses and make us aware of them.

And, most importantly, they do not judge us.

Teacher: Perfect.

What's stopping you from doing that to yourself?

Student: Because I live inside my own head, which is always so cluttered and filled with self-doubt.

There is only one person stopping you from being your own best friend: the person in the mirror.

Teacher: Here are some things that might help.

First, treat yourself the way you would treat your best friend.

Before you begin to spiral in your own thoughts, ask yourself, 'Would I say this to my best friend?'

Student: What do you mean?

Teacher: Imagine your friend accidentally fell down. You gave him a hand, and as soon as he got up, would you ever say, 'You are so stupid. You always make a fool of yourself. Look at all the people laughing at you. You are insufferable'?

Student: That would be a really mean thing to say.

Teacher: And yet we say this to ourselves whenever we fall and bear the responsibility of raising ourselves up.
Why do you think we do that?

Student: Because if I don't, someone else will.

Teacher: Shouldn't it be the opposite?
Irrespective of what you do, there will always be someone seeing the worst in you and calling you out for that.

Why would you do that to yourself before them?

Do not dismiss yourself because, as it is, the world will do everything to dismiss you.

Student: That's so true.

Teacher: Next, help yourself the way you would help your best friend.

You are always there for your best friend, right?

If they seek your help, you offer it.

If they seek validation, you provide it.

If they seek love, you express it.

Stand in front of the mirror and offer the same.

Something as basic as smiling at yourself in the mirror every day.

Look into your eyes and just smile.

Something within you will smile back.

It can't be described, but it is a wonderful feeling.

Student: When you said it, it felt like a warm hug.

Teacher: I am glad you feel that way.
Next, have the ability to laugh at yourself.
Think about it this way – if you show to the world your flaws before they point them out, they are left with nothing to troll.
It is immensely liberating.

Student: But why would I want to do that?
Doesn't this mean that you are exposing your weaknesses upfront?

Teacher: What do you think will make you win in life?
Building on your strengths or hiding your weaknesses?

Student: The way you ask the question – the answer is clear.

Teacher: Your strengths will always offer you significantly more of an advantage than your weaknesses can take away from you.

Being aware of your weaknesses, being comfortable with them will make you respect yourself.

And you know what happens when you respect yourself?

Student: The world also respects you.

Teacher: The world's opinion about us is a reflection of our own opinion about ourselves. This one truth defines all of our interactions in the world.

Student: It is a powerful way to look at relationships.

Teacher: It is indeed.

The next thing to do to become your best friend is to spend time with yourself.

Seek solitude.

Do not seek distraction from your thoughts by running towards people and things. Instead, as hard as it may be, spend time with your own thoughts.

Doing nothing but just thinking.

Student: Is this meditation?

Teacher: You can call it what you want.
It could be meditation. It could be journaling as well. It could be you simply staring into the empty night every day before you hit the bed. The hardest person to spend time with is yourself.
If you become comfortable doing so, you begin to accept yourself for who you are.

Student: I certainly find it therapeutic to spend time with myself. I just didn't realize it would help me get to a good relationship with myself!

Teacher: Which brings me to the last step towards becoming your own friend.
Do not make anybody else responsible for your happiness.
YOU are responsible for your happiness.
So you make that happen.

This means knowing how to have fun with your own self.

This means finding joy in the things you do.

This means seeking a partner not to find happiness in them but rather to share happiness with them.

Student: Wow. This hit hard.

As you say this, I realize in all my relationships, I have blamed the other person for my sadness. I don't feel good about this now.

Teacher: Now go fix it.

It is nobody's job to keep you happy.

If you cannot do it for yourself, it will be exhausting for someone else to keep trying.

Student: Is this why people have run away from me all these years?

Is this why I have lost friends and lovers?

Teacher: It is exhausting to love someone who doesn't love themselves.

Because they never believe that someone can love them so much.

This is why people gravitate towards toxic relationships, toxic friendships because they think they don't deserve better.

That this is the best they can get.

NOT TRUE.

We accept the love we think we deserve.

The day we start loving ourselves, we raise the bar for the one we fall in love with.

Student (crying): It suddenly makes sense.
My entire life makes sense.
This conversation explained everything that I have struggled to understand all these years.
All my life, I have settled for what I thought I deserved, never ever standing up for my own self.
I don't have anyone any more to blame for my state.
I wouldn't even blame myself because, hey, I wouldn't blame my best friend.
I will just pick myself up.
And face tomorrow with a new me!
Will you help me on that journey, please?

Teacher (smiling): You don't need anyone.
The teacher has appeared!

EPILOGUE

Ruchi and I met on a bus.

True story!

I was this geeky kid, obsessed with physics and very clear about what I wanted to do in life. The guy with the plan.

And she?

She was the cool kid. The one always smiling, laughing.

The one, I would argue, I would never want to hang out with.

Because here was someone without a plan, without any visible goal, without a sense of control over her life.

The exact opposite of me!

After college, she worked for 8 years.

And then quit to travel.

Then became a full-time mother for 3 years.

Then decided to represent creative outfits as their sales agent.

Then worked for an organic farm, helping people build a sustainable livelihood.

Then one day, I asked her if she could become my manager.

She said yes.

So today she is my manager.

She is someone without a plan, without any visible goal.

But I was wrong about one thing.

She never lost control over her life.

This is her life.

Fluid.

We have been together for 20+ years now, and the only thing she ever wanted in life was to be happy.

Even when we had no money, even when we had a lot of it.

Even when things were tough, even when they were a joyride.

That was always a choice she exercised. And still continues to.

To be happy.

She is the happiest person I know.

Bubbs and I went to business school together.

She was the first lawyer I had ever met.

But there was something even more fascinating about her.

She was from Goa!

As dumb as it sounds, I never imagined people came from Goa.

It seemed like the place people go to for a vacation.

But here she was, a native, reflecting all the possible Goan traits that I have come to realize are core to them.

Post our MBA, she went to Dubai for her job.

She worked intensely hard, discovered herself, and made a lot of money.

But she craved for home.

So she decided to come back to Goa.

Got a job and did amazing work there.

And one day, she decided to quit all that to move to the development sector.

From a highly paid job, she moved to Delhi, earning 1/20th of what she would get in the market.

I imagined this would perturb her. But it somehow didn't.

She was wonderfully comfortable with the journey she was on.

It took her time. She started from scratch and slowly made it to the top.

But she craved for home.
So she quit again and came back to Goa.

Today she is home.
She works on her own time, spends time with friends and family, chooses not to participate in the corporate rat race.
I find her wonderfully comfortable with where she is.
I think she has found home.

She is the most (I don't know what the word for her is, so let's call her) wonderfully at-peace-with-herself person I know.

I was introduced to Bali through a professor at a Gurugram business school.
He was running his first start-up.
A hustler to the core.
He loved the fight.
He loved the challenge.
And he gave the impression that he could achieve anything he set his mind on.
Which, I have come to realize, is true.

The start-up didn't work out so well, so he joined other start-ups and continued to garner entrepreneurial experience.

He then decided to apply to the Indian School of Business (ISB).

And he got through!

Post ISB, he decided to start up again.

And he did.

He wanted to raise funds from marquee investors.

And he did.

He had multiple near-death experiences in his start-ups.

But he survived.

He felt he should buy his investors out and run his start-up differently.

So he did.

He realized he had to make his start-up profitable to make it last.

So he did.

He did everything that he set his mind on.

He is the best hustler I know.

Singla was presenting at a start-up event when I met him for the first time.

He was impatient with his responses, even with others' questions.

Because he knew his shit!

He always knew his shit!

I found it endearing. Admirable is the right word here.

Lawyers were not known to become entrepreneurs.

Definitely not after quitting a fancy London law firm job!

Bali, Singla and I got close.

He pivoted his start-up.

Raised money from top investors.

And eventually sold his company to Amazon.

Actually let me put that another way.

Amazon, one of the world's most technology-driven companies, bought an Indian start-up founded by a lawyer!

That shit doesn't happen often.

Today, Singla is making a movie.

Because he loves the craft.

And he has a knack for cinema.

And he has understood it, like he has been in
it for decades.
He knows his shit!

Who knows what he will end up doing next?
He is the most meticulous person I know.

I met Chishti when she was a student at ISB.
Like a lot of her batchmates, she too wished
to become a product manager.
Except there were a few problems.
She was not an engineer.
Her previous work experience wasn't the
quintessential product management profile.
And here she was, competing with the best
that the country had to offer.

She got a break at an emerging start-up as a
product manager.
Immediately she found herself in deep water.
Surrounded by smart engineers who talked
in a language that she hadn't learnt or been
exposed to.
So she did what she does best.

She went back to the basics.
Dug into textbooks.
Worked hard.
Through this journey, she joined a deep-tech company.
There was not a single easy day for her.
Her only resolve? Work hard!

Realizing that she needed to prepare herself for a bigger playground she applied to US universities for yet another master's programme.
Got through Berkeley.
The schedule was gruelling, the pressure intense.
And whenever she found herself in shit, she went back to the thing she did best – work hard. Somewhere in that 2-year journey, she ended up writing in her notebook, 'I will be a PM at Google.'

Today, she is a PM at Google, San Francisco.

She is the most hard-working person I know.

These 5 individuals are my closest friends.
They are so different from each other.
So different from me.
But they teach me.
They inspire me.

I share their stories at the end of this book to show how we all have different paths.
We are all different.
However, our definition of success is often twisted by what the world lays down for us.
And it is often a similar definition of success.
Money, Status, Designation.
In chasing that success, we fail to recognize that there are different means to reach the same destination that we find others have reached.

Ruchi chose happiness, Bubbs chose home.
Bali chose hustle, Singla chose rigour, Chishti chose hard work.
But one thing binds them all – they know what works for them.

We all have that power. We all have that choice.
To choose what works for us.
To help us get epic shit done.

The questions I will leave you with are:
What will you choose for yourself?
What will make your teacher appear?

Go GET EPIC SHIT DONE, my friend!
I am excited for you :)

ankur warikoo, signing off.

ACKNOWLEDGEMENTS

This book would not have been possible without Chiki, who convinced me to write another book after *DO EPIC SHIT*, and sought my promise to write one every year. So, I already know that my next book will be out in December 2023 and will be titled *MAKE EPIC MONEY*.

Thanks for pushing me, Chiki.

The entire Juggernaut team, who worked tirelessly and against time to make this book happen.

Nishtha, the one who actually wrote this book. We spent three months on multiple Zoom calls in a dialogue similar to how you read it in the book. She pretended to be the student and I acted as the teacher. Those meetings were recorded, translated into words, then a structure and eventually this book.

And all of that is her work.

I owe the book to her.

She put everything she had into it, and I hope you appreciate the hard work just as much as I witnessed it.

Finally, Supriya, whose lovely illustrations lend weight to the words you have read. She is wonderful at her work, and I love the simplicity of her visual communication.

There are so many others to thank.

You all know who you are.

I hope you know there is never a moment I am not grateful to have you in my life.

I rest on the shoulders of others.

And for that, I will forever be obliged.

A NOTE ON THE AUTHOR

Ankur Warikoo is an internet entrepreneur based out of India and is one of the country's top content creators. His first book, *DO EPIC SHIT*, went on to become a bestseller. Besides creating content for his 7M+ audience across social media, Ankur conducts online courses as an educator through his current start-up, WebVeda.

In his spare time, Ankur loves to mentor entrepreneurs and is also an active angel investor. Previously, he founded nearbuy.com and was its CEO from its inception in 2015 until 2019. Prior to that, Ankur was the founding CEO of Groupon's India business in 2011.

Ankur was part of *Fortune* magazine's 40 Under 40 list for India; *Forbes India*'s Top 100 Digital Creators list for 2022; LinkedIn India's Top Voices for 2018, 2019 and 2020; LinkedIn India's Spotlight list and *Business Today*'s list of India's Top Executives Under 40.

You can connect with him on Twitter @warikoo, on YouTube @warikoo and on Instagram on @ankurwarikoo.

juggernaut

THE APP FOR INDIAN READERS

Fresh, original books tailored for mobile and for India. Starting at ₹10.

juggernaut.in

To download the app scan the QR Code
with a QR scanner app

For our complete catalogue, visit www.juggernaut.in
To submit your book, send a synopsis and two
sample chapters to books@juggernaut.in
For all other queries, write to contact@juggernaut.in